Environment, Natural Resources and the Indian Economy

Environment, Natural Resources and the Indian Economy

Editors

Amarendra Das • Padmaja Mishra

UTKAL UNIVERSITY

Department of Analytical and Applied Economics,
(UGC Centre of Advanced Study in Economics),
Utkal University, Bhubaneswar

in association with

New Century Publications
New Delhi, India

NEW CENTURY PUBLICATIONS
4800/24, Bharat Ram Road,
Ansari Road, Daryaganj,
New Delhi - 110 002 (India)

Tel.: 011-2324 7798, 4358 7398, 6539 6605
Fax: 011-4101 7798
E-mail: indiatax@vsnl.com • info@newcenturypublications.com
www.newcenturypublications.com

Editorial office:
LG–7, Aakarshan Bhawan,
4754-57/23, Ansari Road, Daryaganj,
New Delhi – 110 002

Tel.: 011-4356 0919

First Published: **July 2014**

ISBN: **978-81-7708-348-4**

Published by New Century Publications and printed at Salasar Imaging Systems, New Delhi.

Designs: Patch Creative Unit, New Delhi.

PRINTED IN INDIA

About the Book

Environmental pollution is one of the major problems faced by the world community, especially in the cities of the developing countries which have experienced unbridled growth of population, urbanization and industrialization.

Soil, forests, mines, water, air and other natural resources are productive assets of an economy. These natural and environmental resources are the basis of all economic activities. Economic activities, in turn, affect the quantity and quality of natural and environmental resources. Mining, lumbering, manufacturing, fishing and a host of other economic activities change the stock of natural resources which calls for appropriate trade-off between the needs of the present and future generations.

India is the second most populous and seventh largest country in the world. Geographically, it accounts for a meagre 2.4 percent of the world's total surface area but supports and sustains a whopping 16.7 percent of the world population.

Environmental problems in India can be classified into two broad categories: (a) those arising from conditions of poverty and under-development, and (b) those arising as negative effects of the very process of development.

The present volume contains 12 research papers—authored by experts in the field of environmental economics—which provide deep insights into the linkages between development and environment and suggest remedial measures for environmentally sustainable economic policies.

About the Editors

Dr. Amarendra Das is Assistant Professor in the Post-graduate Department of Analytical and Applied Economics, Utkal University, Bhubaneswar, Odisha. He is currently on deputation to the Fourteenth Finance Commission of India as Deputy Director. He obtained his M.A. in Analytical and Applied Economics from Utkal University, and M.Phil. in Applied Economics and Ph.D. in Economics from the Centre for Development Studies, Thiruvananthapuram [under Jawaharlal Nehru University (JNU)], New Delhi. He won Global Development Medal for the year 2008 sponsored by Global Development Network. He has published several articles in various reputed journals and books. His research and teaching interest lies in natural resource management, environmental economics, public finance and international trade.

Dr. Padmaja Mishra is currently Professor in the Post-graduate Department of Analytical and Applied Economics, Utkal University, Bhubaneswar, Odisha. She did her Masters and M.Phil. in Economics from Utkal University. She has been a Commonwealth Academic Staff Scholar and received her Ph.D. from the University of East Anglia, U.K. She has pursued her post-doctoral work at the University of Maryland, U.S.A. She is a member of the Regional Direct Tax Advisory Committee and the State Level Expert Appraisal Committee for Environment Impact Assessment. Economics of environment is one of her favourite areas of teaching and research. She has many national and international publications to her credit and continues to guide M.Phil. and Ph.D. works in economics.

Contents

Contributors

M.N. Murty	Professor (Retired) and Senior Consultant at Institute of Economic Growth (IEG), Delhi.
Sarmila Banerjee	Rajiv Gandhi Chair Professor, Department of Economics, University of Calcutta, Kolkata.
P.P. Mitra	Chief Economic Adviser, Ministry of Rural Development, Government of India.
N.K. Sahu	Economic Adviser, Ministry of Rural Development, Government of India.
Mahipal	Director, Ministry of Rural Development, Government of India.
Mukesh Kumar	Assistant Commissioner, Ministry of Rural Development, Government of India.
Sanatan Nayak	Associate Professor, Department of Economics, B.B. Ambedkar University, Lucknow.
Surajit Haldar	Assistant Professor in Agricultural Economics, College of Horticulture, Sambalpur, Odisha.
Honnaiah	Associate Professor, Department of Agricultural Economics, University of Agricultural Sciences, Bangalore.
Sowmyashree B.V.	Research Assistant at ADRTC, Institute for Social and Economic Change (ISEC), Bangalore.
Abhiram Dash	Assistant Professor, College of Agriculture, Orissa University of Agriculture and Technology, Sambalpur, Odisha.
Jeeban Jyoti Mohanty	Ph.D. Scholar, Department of Economics, Ravenshaw University, Cuttack, Odisha.
Sibananda Senapati	Research Scholar at National Institute of Industrial Engineering (NITIE), Mumbai.

Vijaya Gupta Associate Professor in Economics, National Institute of Industrial Engineering (NITIE), Mumbai.

Suman Devi Research Scholar, Department of Humanities and Social Sciences, National Institute of Technology (NIT), Rourkela, Odisha.

Nihar Ranjan Mishra Assistant Professor, Department of Humanities and Social Sciences, National Institute of Technology (NIT), Rourkela, Odisha.

Raghunath Sahoo Assistant Professor in Economics, Department of Management Studies, Apex Institute of Technology and Management, Bhubaneswar, Odisha.

Mamata Swain Professor, Post-graduate Department of Economics, Ravenshaw University, Cuttack, Odisha.

K.A. Mohammed Noushad Chief Conservator of Forests, Kerala Forest Department, Kollam, Kerala.

Ashok Kumar Maurya Research Scholar, Centre for Studies in Economics and Planning, School of Social Science, Central University of Gujarat, Gandhinagar, Gujarat.

Kalpana Sahoo Doctoral Research Fellow (JRF), Department of Humanities and Social Sciences, National Institute of Technology (NIT), Rourkela, Odisha.

Narayan Sethi Assistant Professor in Economics, Department of Humanities and Social Sciences, National Institute of Technology (NIT), Rourkela, Odisha.

Introduction

Amarendra Das and Padmaja Mishra

Environmental sustainability is a central part of sustainable development. Natural resources need to complement man made resources continuously for an uninterrupted economic growth. Unfortunately, per capita availability of natural resources is declining because of growing population and unscrupulous resource exploitation by human beings. Resources like land, fresh water and minerals are limited and scarce. Renewable resources like forests and fisheries are harvested at an unsustainable rate. The rate of pollution generation has exceeded the assimilation capacity of the nature. Scientists have converged in their view that the rise in the temperature of the Earth is induced by anthropogenic activities. Global warming and climate changes are posing serious threats to economic growth and poverty reduction. How do we manage our environment and natural resources for sustained economic growth, development and human well-being?

In the traditional Indian society, the use of environmental resources like air, water, soil was governed by the religious beliefs and norms. However, with the spread of modernity in Indian society, people violated such beliefs and norms and started abusing these resources. In order to fulfill the consumption requirements of burgeoning population, natural resources are being overexploited. Starting from early 1970s, it was felt, at global and national level that we cannot take the environment and nature for granted. We need to have certain fundamental principles for using the environment and natural resources. This is witnessed from the discussions held at two important international conferences on environment and development—one at Stockholm in 1972 and another at Rio de Janeiro in 1992—which have influenced environmental policies in most countries, including India. The World

Commission on Environment and Development (1987) recognized that the environment and natural resources are not meant for the consumption of present generation only. Rather they ought to be left in the same amount for the future generations. Thus, it stressed upon achieving sustainable development and defined sustainable development as 'development that meets the needs of the present without compromising the ability of the future generation to meet their own needs'.

A slew of legislations have been enacted and policies have been announced in India for the better management of natural resources and environmental conservation. A few such legislations are as follows:

- Mines and Minerals (Regulation and Development) Act, 1957.
- Wild Life (Protection) Act, 1972.
- Water (Prevention and Control of Pollution) Act, 1974
- Forest (Conservation) Act, 1980.
- Air (Prevention and Control of Pollution) Act, 1981.
- Environment (Protection) Act 1986.
- Public Liability Insurance Act, 1991.
- National Environment Tribunal Act, 1995.

Although there are many rules and regulations and institutions to manage the environmental resources of the country, the enforcement of these laws has failed miserably. Nevertheless, the awareness of individuals on environmental problems has been growing. In this context, this edited volume compiles together 12 research papers (chapters) on various issues pertaining to environment and natural resources.

Chapter 1 discusses Green GDP accounting and mentions that development of aggregate national income accounts for measuring Green GDP requires a bottom up approach. Development of physical accounts of environmental changes could be possible only at project or sector level while the aggregate monetary accounts could be developed for the economy as a whole. While discussing some conceptual problems of aggregation of physical and monetary accounts of environmental changes at micro level, this chapter provides insights into data requirements and the problems of measurement with help of case studies of air pollution abatement in India.

Chapter 2 examines the effects of trade liberalization on the environment of India. The author argues that for a country like India, where a large part of production is organized in the informal sector, it is doubtful whether introduction of uniform regulation would lead to adoption of cleaner production techniques in the formal sector or create an escape route to outsource polluting processes to informal sector units and retain the cost competitiveness in the world market. Thus, in the presence of regulatory leakages, trade liberalization might impose significant environmental costs on the economy and make the process of rapid growth unsustainable in the long-run. It is interesting to note that the share of dirty exports [1] in India's total exports is very high and has hovered around 65-70 percent throughout, across both pre- and post-liberalization as well as pre- and post-WTO regimes. Since India has experienced commendable export growth in the post-liberalization period, such high share of dirty exports might impose significant environmental costs on the economy unless the WTO norms encourage adoption of cleaner production and abatement techniques. Hence, the moot point is whether the source of this competitive advantage of India in the international market is located in her structural strength or weakness? In case of former, the trade-led growth will be sustainable in the long-run but in case of latter, the economic prosperity and environmental sustainability may move in opposite direction.

The author focuses on the gems and jewelry industry of India and points out that the root of competitive advantage of our leading export sectors may be located in the structural weakness of the economy and, if so, the recently experienced high growth may not be sustainable in the long-run. Hence, to ensure sustainable long-run growth in a globally integrated world, the policy planners need to pay more attention to address the bottlenecks imposed by the inherent features of underdevelopment by designing suitable instruments for intervention.

Chapter 3 presents the conceptual framework and empirical evidence of measuring green outcomes of rural development programmes in India. The efficacy of rural development programmes, apart from poverty alleviation among others, is also measured by the green outcomes of such programmes since the issue of sustainable development, keeping in view the need to protect and rejuvenate environment, has become paramount in the development agenda.

A format for water accounting as adopted in some countries has also been discussed and an attempt has been made to find a proxy for shadow prices, which is the amount of money spent from the public exchequer per unit of water consumed by the society. It has been suggested that rural development programmes in India which have water conservation as one of their objectives should have an elaborate water accounting framework, which would be useful to compute shadow prices of water and pinpoint the green outcomes of rural development programmes.

Chapter 4 presents the benefits of sodic reclamation on the economic sustainability of agriculture in Uttar Pradesh. The study presents an account of the changing scenario of the cropping pattern, production, productivity, net gain under reclaimed conditions compared to that of non-reclaimed conditions. Further, employment generation in the reclaimed and non-reclaimed villages are also covered under this study. The productivity of various important crops clearly reveals that there has been a substantial improvement of per acre production in reclaimed land over the non-reclaimed land in the villages sampled for the study. However, the productivity of the reclaimed land for various major crops is still lower than the productivity of normal land.

Further, the study reveals that family labour has larger share for any kind of crops in both reclaimed as well as non-reclaimed land. The per acre family labour for all other crops except paddy has increased in reclaimed land over non-reclaimed land. Moreover, per acre hired labour is lower than that of family labour in both reclaimed and non-reclaimed land.

Chapter 5 provides an economic analysis of cutting edge technology in rice cultivation with special reference to system of rice intensification (SRI) method in West Bengal. SRI has been practiced since decades with multi-purpose benefits of higher yield with qualitative gains and fodder production that confer a degree of protection against climatic hazards and losses against pests and diseases. The comparative economic analysis of SRI and conventional method of rice cultivation was assessed based on the primary survey during 2009-10 in Bardhaman district of West Bengal.

SRI farmers were found to be technically more efficient than conventional rice farmers in terms of sustainable ground water usage and extraction. The logit analysis results revealed that the probability of adoption of SRI increases with the literacy level. Difficulties in management practices like water management, inter-cultural operations due to lack of skilled labour and water scarcity during *rabi* season were the major factors that limit the wide scale adoption of SRI method.

Chapter 6 examines the potential and constraints of organic farming through a study carried out in Keonjhar district of Odisha. Besides, the study has also made an attempt to understand the feasibility of the organic farming in Odisha. Different methodologies have been used to satisfy the various objectives of the study. To understand the macro factors affecting the organic farming, both primary and secondary data were used. Further, the study undertook a case study to know the situation at ground level.

The study finds that the greatest impact of organic agriculture is on the mindset of the people. By adopting organic agriculture, farmers are challenged to take on new knowledge and perspective and to innovate. This leads to an increased engagement in farming which can trigger greater opportunity for rural development and economic upliftment.

Chapter 7 discusses the climate change vulnerability and livelihood sustainability in coastal regions of India with reference to fishing communities of Mumbai. Sea level rise (SLR) and coastal flooding remain major challenges for the entire densely populated coasts of India that supports a number of economic activities. The fishing communities who live very close to the sea happen to be the worst affected. The livelihood of fishermen is vulnerable, both economically and socially, to such changes. In this context, the chapter highlights the social-economic issues due to climate change among the fishing communities in India. The chapter also presents a case study of fishing community (popularly known as Koli) of Mumbai. Five fishing villages (known as Koliwada) of Mumbai were selected for primary data collection. Primary data collected from a sample of 182 households was statistically analysed for socio-economic issues, the perception of fishermen towards climate change, their adaptation measures, and government support etc. The analysis revealed that the changing climate pattern is affecting fishing communities, fish catch and thus their livelihood.

Chapter 8 focuses on the community participation in common property resource (CPR) management by undertaking a study of one watershed project. It is argued that judicious use of CPR is necessary for a developing country like India. Their mismanagement has serious implications on both environment and people. Towards this end, Watershed Development Programmes (WSDP) implemented by the Government, NGOs and other external agencies adopted a participatory approach. Watershed is a special type of CPR. However, much controversy has been raised over local community involvement in managing CPRs. Many successful Watershed Management Programmes—such as Ralegaon Sidhi, Adgaon (Maharashtra), Sukhomajiri (Haryana) and Jhabua (Madhya Pradesh)—have shown that community participation is crucial to the success of these programmes. The study uses sociological and anthropological tools and techniques for narrating the field experience, and findings from available literature and reports. The author observed that community participation in CPRs is determined by many situations. Immediate economic gain attracts the community for participation. Other factors that influence the community participation are socio-economic conditions such as equal distribution of benefits, and good rapport with project implementing agencies (PIAs).

Chapter 9 attempts to analyze the benefits accrued to the forest dwellers from their participation in the management of common property resources (CPRs) namely joint forest management (JFM). The study among four villages in Keonjhar district of Odisha covered 200 households (105 JFM households and 95 Non-JFM households) comprising of landless and agricultural labourers, marginal and small farmers (poor households), and medium and large farmers (non-poor households). The household level benefits in terms of employment generation, income from timber and non-timber forest products (NTFP), and fuel wood collection from community managed forests to the households participating in JFM are higher than that that for non-participating (in JFM) households. It was found that the income and employment opportunities for the poor households have increased more compared to the non-poor households in the study area since the establishment of JFM. Measures need to be undertaken to ensure retention, regeneration and sustainable utilization of forests to provide livelihood security to the forest dependent rural communities.

Chapter 10 presents the issues and concerns in management of non-timber forest produces in Kerala and suggests the remedial measures. The once mangrove rich coastal belts are impoverished due to intensive agriculture, urbanisation and developmental activities. Shrinking resource base, escalating demand and over exploitation are the major concerns of conservation. The author suggests that as future yield from the wild will not match up to the demand, in situ conservation has to be complemented by ex-situ methods. The escalating demand can be met only by collaborative efforts of forest department, industry and farmers, along with the application of frontier technologies and optimal utilization of resources.

Chapter 11 discusses about the drinking water schemes for the effective management of surface water resources in North Gujarat. Water has become a scarce commodity today and defines human, social and economic development. Without adequate supplies and management of freshwater resources, socio-economic development cannot take place. The author points out that Gujarat is a water scarce state and confronting big problem due to worst water quality like saline and fluoride contaminated groundwater. Presently, various surface water schemes are running in Gujarat and a major part of North Gujarat is covered by Narmada canal.

Chapter 12 presents an empirical analysis of the impact of foreign aid on environmental quality in India. It examines the impact of foreign assistance on environmental quality in India by using the Granger causality technique for the time period 1970-71 to 2010-11. The Granger causality test shows that foreign aid, population growth, urbanization and economic growth are significant determinants of environmental quality in India.

Acknowledgements

We place on record our deep appreciation for all the scholars who have contributed to this volume. Their research findings will surely add to the existing body of literature on interface between environment and development. We express our deep sense of gratitude to the Department of Economic Affairs, Ministry of Finance, Government of India, for providing the funds. At last, but most importantly, we would also like to thank New Century Publications, New Delhi for publishing this edited volume.

Endnote

1. Dirty commodities among India's major export items were identified as those classified as Red and Orange category dirty industries by the Central Pollution Control Board (CPCB) and accepted by the Central Statistical Organization (CSO) of India to identify dirty production in manufacturing sector (Chaudhuri and Ray, 2000).

Bhubaneswar

Amarendra Das
Padmaja Mishra

1

Micro Foundations of Measuring Green GDP

M.N. Murty

Introduction

Measurement of net national product (NNP) taking into account the externalities of using natural resources requires the generalization of conventional national income accounts to be done for the economy. Some of these generalizations could be already found in the UN Methodology of Integrated Environmental and Economic Accounting (UN, 1993) and in recent attempts for developing environmentally extended input-output models (EU, 2005). However, there is a large gap between what is empirically achieved so far and the requirement of these generalized methods of accounting. These methods require an aggregation of changes in natural resource stocks at the micro level or an aggregation of changes over the firms and households to arrive at changes at the level of sectors and from the sector to the macro or national level aggregates. There are formidable empirical problems in measuring the changes in resource stocks introduced by firms or projects and the monetary valuation of these changes.

The general view about sustainable income is that it is the maximum attainable income in one period with the guarantee that the same level of income will be available in future periods given the constraints on the resources, viz. labour, man-made capital and natural capital. Therefore, income is directly related to the availability of man-made and natural capital. Sustainable income defined in this way represents the welfare of the nation and there is a lot of discussion in the literature about whether the net national product (NNP) would appropriately represent it. [1]

It is long recognized that the conventional system of national accounts (SNA) to measure NNP has treated environmental resources and their role in the economy inconsistently. Under SNA, NNP increases when natural resource stocks are depleted and the quality of environment is reduced by pollution. The correct approach to natural resources accounting is to account for the depletion of natural resources and the fall in the environmental quality in estimating the NNP. [2] In a free market situation, there may not be adequate incentives for the economic activities to account for the depletion of natural resources caused by them. The environmental regulation with the appropriate instruments and institutions could provide sufficient incentives for profit maximizing activities for the sustainable use of natural resources.

Accounting Principles for Environmental Resources and Green GDP

Natural resources are classified as renewable and exhaustible in resource economics with different accounting principles for measuring their contribution to net national product (NNP). [3]

Accounting Principles for Renewable Resources: Given that environmental resources are renewable, the change in the environmental resource stock, ΔS_t during a given time, say a year, is estimated as:

$$\Delta S_t = N(S_t) - E_t + A_t \qquad (2.1)$$

where (S_t), the stock of environmental resource (quality of water resources or atmosphere) at time t; $N(S_t)$ the natural rate of regeneration of this stock (natural rate of assimilation of pollution loads); (E_t), the rate of depletion of stock (rate of degradation of environmental quality); and (A_t), the rate of pollution abatement. The environmentally corrected net national product (ENNP) with the sustainable use of environmental resources could be estimated as:

$$ENNP=C_t+\Delta K_t+M'\Delta S_t \quad (2.2)$$

where (C_t), is the consumption, (ΔK_t), the value of change in manmade capital or investment, (ΔS_t), the change in environmental capital and $M(A_t)$ and (M') are respectively the pollution abatement cost function and the marginal cost of pollution abatement. The accounting principle therefore is to evaluate the changes in environmental resource stocks at the marginal costs of avoiding the depletion of the stocks. The marginal cost of avoiding the depletion is the price of an environmental resource in the context of sustainable development.

Accounting Principles for Exhaustible Resources: Extraction of exhaustible natural resources like fossil fuels, minerals, metals and ores and their use in various economic activities has implications for sustainable development in two important ways: inter-generational equity and environmental degradation. Given the property right of an exhaustible resource to the present and future generations, sustainable development has to ensure just distribution of benefits from the resource to present and future generations. Exploitation of exhaustible resources contributes to environmental degradation. Mining of resources could result in deforestation, land degradation and water and air pollution which could be identified by attempting full life cycle analysis of resource use. Accounting principles require first establishment of the change in the stock of exhaustible resources during the accounting period and the monetary value of this stock from the inter-generational equity point of view. Also, it is required to find out the change in the environmental resource stocks consequent to the extraction of exhaustible resources in the accounting period and the monetary value of this change.

Changes in the resource stocks in this context have to be estimated as follows:

The rate of depletion of the resource stock ΔR, if fresh discoveries of the resource are not there, is given by:

$$\Delta R, = -Y_t, \tag{2.3}$$

where R_t and Y_t represent respectively, the stock of exhaustible resource, say coal and the amount of resource extracted. The rate of depletion of environmental resource stock ΔS_t consequent on the extraction of exhaustible resource is given by:

$$\Delta S_t = N(S_t) - \alpha\, Y_t + A_t, \tag{2.4}$$

where A_t is the rate of pollution abatement and α is the rate of environmental resource degradation per unit extraction of Y_t. The environmentally corrected net national product (ENNP) with the sustainable use of exhaustible resources could be estimated as,

$$ENNP = C_t + \Delta K + M'\Delta S + \{((F_y - v_t) - \alpha M')\}R_t. \tag{2.5}$$

where F_y and v_t are respectively value of marginal product of resource and per unit cost of resource extraction.

The first four components are the same as those in equation (2.2). The term $[(F_y - v_t) - \alpha M')]$ in the equation could be interpreted as the generalized Hotelling rent on an exhaustible resource after accounting for the cost of avoiding environmental degradation arising out of use of the resource. By using say one tonne of fossil fuel, α tons of pollution is generated and the cost of abatement of it is $\alpha\, M'$ which has to be accounted in defining the Hotelling rent. It is so because the cost of depletion of environmental quality due to pollution evaluated at the shadow price, the marginal cost of pollution abatement, is already accounted in measuring ENNP through the third component in equation (2.5).

Integrated Economic and Environmental Accounting

Measurement of environmental costs and benefits of sustainable development requires measurement of the effects of development activities on the natural resource stocks in the economy. As discussed in the above section, measurement of national income with sustainable development requires the identification of aggregate changes in the natural resource stocks and the monetary valuation of these during the given accounting period. The UN Methodology [4] of Integrated Environmental and Economic Accounting recognizes this and suggests the development of physical and monetary accounts of natural resource stocks as a satellite system to a core system of conventional national income accounts. There are two important steps in the development of integrated economic and environmental accounting: first, namely the description of stocks of natural assets in physical terms and the measurement of changes in stocks during the accounting period; and the second is the valuation of natural assets. Natural assets provide both marketable and non-marketable services and therefore their valuation requires the use of market and non-market valuation techniques.

The development of integrated environmental and economic accounts starts with the description of two proto types of environmental accounting in physical terms: material energy balances and natural resource accounting. Material and energy balance accounting shows raw materials as inputs, transformation process in the economy, and flows of residuals resulting from the economic uses of materials back to the environment. Transformation processes within the natural environment are excluded. Natural resource accounting describes the stocks and stock changes of natural assets, comprising biological assets (produced or wild), sub-soil assets (proved reserves), water, air and land areas with their terrestrial and aquatic ecosystems. Biological natural assets consist of plants and animals of economic importance. Land areas include area as well as related biological ecosystems. Sub-soil assets consist only of proved reserves. Water and air are accounted in so far as they are used or are affected by the economic activities.

The methods of valuation of environmental services could be classified as three different valuation types: (a) market valuation according to the concept of the non-financial asset accounts in the conventional system of national accounts, (b) maintenance valuation, which estimates the cost necessary to sustain at least the present level of natural assets, and (c) non-market valuation using hypothetical behavioral methods: contingent valuation methods and the observed behavioral methods such as hedonic prices, travel cost and household production functions for estimating the value of consumptive services of the natural environment.

The maintenance valuation method uses actual or hypothetical cost data. Expenditures required for maintaining the services of natural environment constitute the actual cost. These are the costs for an increase in environmental protection activities that prevent the degradation of natural assets. These could be interpreted as the value that the producer or polluter places on the environmental services he receives. The hypothetical cost of using environment is the cost that would have been incurred if the environment had been used in such a way that would not affect its future use. The rationale behind using this method of valuation is the concept of sustainable income discussed in the earlier sections.

Estimation of values that the households place on environmental services requires the use of non-market valuation methods. There is a lot of literature now about the use of these methods for estimating the household values of environmental resources (Freeman, 1993; Mitchell and Carson, 1989; Murty and Surender Kumar, 2004). The hypothetical behavioral methods comprising contingent valuation and other variants of this can be used to measure both user and non-user benefits from environmental resources. The observed behavioral methods indirectly use market information to estimate user benefits.

Environmental Extensions of Input-output Tables

SEEA provides a conceptual base for the environmental extensions of input-output table (EEIOT). Mainly two types of extensions could be distinguished.

1. Natural resources covering mineral and energy resources, water and biological resources flow form the natural environment into national economy.
2. Residuals consisting of emissions to air, water and soil are the incidental and undesired outputs from the economy discharged into the environment.

Applications of an EEIOT:

1. Environmental problem analysis: Analysis of the nature and causes of environmental problems, as related to resource use and emissions relevant for policy. For example, it includes the analysis of life cycle environmental impacts of product groups (cars, meat, houses etc.), consumer groups (urban versus rural dwellers), and impacts related to primary resources used (oil, iron ore, coal, wood etc.).
2. Prospective Effect Analysis of Policies: Ex-ante prediction of effects of policy measures. These include economy-wise environmental implications of changes in lifestyles and consumption expenditure patterns, technological changes of products and processes, emission reduction measures, and price effects of environmental taxation and other ways of internalizing the environmental externalities.
3. Monitoring and ex-post effect analysis of policies: Ex-post analysis of impacts and effectiveness of policy measures. It involves the analysis of relationship between environmental impact (emissions, material requirement) and economic output. Standard IO notation (matrices in capital, vectors in lower case).

Environmental Accounting for Thermal Power Sector

Introduction: Natural environment provides waste disposal services as productive inputs to industry. Given the environmental regulation, producers place a value on these inputs similar to the way they value other conventional inputs such as labour, man-made capital and materials. Environmental regulation meant for ensuring an environmentally sustainable industrial development imposes a cost on the industry. The UN Methodology for an Integrated Environmental and Economic Accounting calls this cost as maintenance cost or the cost to the industry for maintaining the quality of environment at its natural regenerative level. A model in the theory of production is used in this study for estimating the maintenance cost.

The model describes the technology of power generation as one of producing jointly, good output, power and bad output, pollution load—using the output distance function. The producer-demand prices for waste disposal services from the environmental media could be defined as the opportunity costs in terms of good output foregone to reduce bad output in this model. In any attempt to measure green GDP, estimates of these prices are needed to value changes in environmental quality caused by the developmental activities. A case study of thermal power generation in Andhra Pradesh in India is done for preparing the physical monetary accounts of environmental pollution at the sectoral level.

Thermal Power Generation in Andhra Pradesh: Andhra Pradesh Power Generation Corporation (APGENCO) (formerly known as Andhra Pradesh State Electricity Board, APSEB) came into existence on February 1, 1999. APGENCO was supposed to acquire the power plants established by APSEB and establish, construct and operate power-generating stations. All the five plants under study are now owned by APGENCO and are subjected to environmental regulations in the generation of power. The corporation has an unwritten environmental policy to comply with the relevant environmental legislations and regulatory requirements for the establishment and operation of the power stations. High efficiency electro-static precipitators (ESPs) are installed to control suspended particulate matter (SPM) in the flue gas. All new plants are designed for the SPM level of 100 mg./NM^3, a limit set by the Andhra Pradesh Pollution Control Board (APPCB). Old units are upgraded or are under upgradation for 50/115 mg./NM^3 against a limit of 115 mg./NM^3. The latest micro processor based EPIC-II controllers are installed for improvement of collection efficiency and a reduction of power consumption. Online flue gas dust monitoring systems are installed in some plants.

In India, the electricity sector is regulated and the state regulatory commissions determine the price of electricity for different categories of consumers accordingly and Andhra Pradesh is no exception. Cross-subsidies are widespread and domestic and agricultural consumers are charged lower prices in comparison to production costs, but commercial and industrial consumers have to pay higher prices.

The output distance function is estimated using data for five coal fired thermal power generating plants belonging to APGENCO. The data set used constitutes a panel consisting of monthly observations on variables during the years 1996-97 to 2003-04. It contains 480 observations on electricity produced, air pollutants SPM, SO_2 and NO_x generated as well as coal and other inputs used by the five electricity generating plants. Electricity generated is considered as a good output while the three pollutants SPM, SO_2 and NO_x generated are taken as bad outputs in the estimation. Table 1.1 provides the descriptive statistic of the variables used in the estimation of the distance function.

For the estimation of shadow prices of bad outputs, we need the information on electricity prices. Here, we are assuming that the price paid by industrial consumers is equal to the price prevalent in a free market as it is safe to assume that industrial consumers are rational decision-makers who have to take decisions for the profit motive. In 2003-04, the industrial consumers were paying ₹ 3.6 per unit of electricity.

The variables used in the study are as below.

SPM, SO2, and NOx: Monthly loads in tonnes discharged by the power plant were computed by multiplying the monthly average concentration of the pollutant (mg./NM^3) with the monthly volume of stack discharge (NM^3) for each plant.

Electricity: Electricity produced by the plant during a year in (million units).

Capital: Capital stock of a plant observed at the beginning of a year which is assumed to be fixed for the rest of the year.

Coal: Annual consumption of coal by the plant (in tonnes).

Wage Bill: Annual wage bill of a plant (in million rupees).

Table 1.1: Descriptive Statistics of the Variables Used in Study

Variable	Unit	Mean	Standard Dev.	Maximum	Minimum
Electricity	Million Units	298.28	13.91	933.58	0.01
SPM	Tonnes	653	0.033	3.526	0.018
SO_2	Tonnes	874	0.049	4.268	0.004
NO_x	Tonnes	139	0.013	1.984	0.001
Coal	Tonnes	223460	9.93	667.05	0.01
Capital	Rupees millions	1913.231	905.46	62395.28	148.59
Wage Bill	Rupees millions	255.628	111.03	9332.04	344.16

Shadow Prices of Pollutants and Pollution Taxes: Using the estimated output distance function, the shadow price of a pollutant is estimated in terms of units of good output foregone for one unit reduction in pollution. The current electricity tariff for industries in AP is on the average ₹ 3.60 per unit. Using this price, shadow prices of pollutants could be expressed in rupees for a representative plant of APGENCO as ₹ 1,043, ₹ 5,867 and ₹ 11,539 respectively per tonne reduction of SPM, NO_x, and SO_2 as reported in Table 1.2.

Table 1.2: Shadow Prices of Pollutants

(₹ per tonne)

Industrial Pollutants	Mean	Standard Deviation
SPM	1,043	1,067
SO_2	5,867	8,706
NO_2	11,539	21,153

Estimation of pollution taxes using the Taxes-Standards method requires estimates of the marginal cost of pollution abatement and the data on pollution standards. The shadow price reported in Table 1.2 could also be interpreted as the marginal costs of pollution abatement. Using the estimated output distance function for thermal power generation in AP, plant-specific shadow prices could be calculated. The marginal cost of pollution abatement for each pollutant could be obtained by finding a relationship between the shadow price of the pollutant and pollution load. The marginal cost of pollution abatement of a plant could depend on output, pollution load and plant-specific characteristics among others.

Cost of Environmentally Sustainable Thermal Power Generation and Measurement of Green GDP: Physical and monetary accounts of air pollution for the thermal power generating sector have to be prepared for estimating the cost of environmentally sustainable power development or the maintenance cost, the cost of maintaining the environmental quality at its natural regenerative level. Scientifically, the environmental standards (Minimum National Standards, MINAS in India or WHO standards) are supposed to be designed taking into account the natural regenerative capacity of the environment media. Therefore, one way of measuring the depletion of air quality from power generation is to consider the difference between the actual pollution load and the pollution load corresponding to the standards. This method of measuring depletion is consistent with the definition of depletion of environmental quality in equation 2.1. Row 2 of Table 1.3 provides estimates of depletion of air quality by a typical plant of APGENCO. Given the shadow prices of air pollutants reported again in row 3 of the same table, the estimates of cost of avoiding this depletion or the cost of complying with the pollution standards for an average plant are estimated as reported in row 4. The annual cost of reducing the pollution levels of SPM, SO_2, and NO_x from the current levels to zero in all plants of APGENCO is estimated as ₹ 534 million. This cost has to be accounted for in the measurement of green GDP or environmentally corrected net national product (ENNP).

Table 1.3: Physical and Monetary Accounts of Air Pollution for APGENCO

	SPM	SO_2	NO_X
Load (tonnes/yr.)	7836	10488	1668
Shadow Price (₹)	1,043	5,867	11,539
Cost of Abatement (₹ million)	8.173	61.533	19.247

Note: Row 2 of table shows the data of observed emissions of SPM, NO_X, and SO_2.

Environmental Accounting for Urban Airsheds

Households place a value on the ambient air quality in urban areas. The physical accounts of air pollution for an urban area describe the ambient air quality during an accounting period. There are MINAS standards in India and WHO standards for ambient urban air quality which are supposed to be fixed by taking into account the carrying capacity of urban air sheds.

The physical accounts describe the excess of ambient air pollution over these standards. Estimates of household values of urban air quality could be used to estimate the damages households receive from the air pollution in excess of safe standards. Some recent studies in India (Murty, Gulati and Banerjee, 2003; Murty and Gulati, 2005) provide estimates of household marginal willingness to pay function for urban air quality improvement in the cities of Delhi, Kolkata and Hyderabad using the hedonic property values method of environmental valuation.

The consumer surplus generated by the reduction of SPM concentration from the current average to the safe level of 200 μ gm/m^3 is computed by integrating the estimate of inverse demand function within 200 μ gm/m^3 as the lower limit [6] and the current average level of pollution in the respective cities as the upper limit. The estimated consumer surplus also measures the average willingness to pay by a representative household for reduction in the ambient air pollution from the current average to the safe WHO or MINAS [7] standards. The annual welfare gains to a typical household from reducing SPM concentration from the current level to the MINAS standard of 200 μ gms/m^3 in Delhi are ₹ 23,354. According to the 2000 census, Delhi has an urban population of 12.8 million with the sample average household size being 5.46. Thus, there are 23,47,942 estimated urban households in Delhi. The annual benefits from reducing the SPM concentration to safe level in Delhi are estimated as ₹ 54,833 million. A similar estimate for the urban area of Kolkata is ₹ 37,026 million. Having these estimates for all the urban areas in India, an estimate of damages from the current levels of urban air pollution could be obtained. The NNP of India corrected for the urban air pollution could be obtained after accounting for these damages in its estimation.

Alternatively, the abatement cost method could be used for the valuation of urban pollution. There could source-specific air pollution standards as described in the earlier section on thermal power generation and the cost of complying with these standards by the polluters could be estimated. Ideally, the source-specific air pollution standards and ambient standards have to be linked in the sense that if the sources comply with the standards, the ambient air quality standards are met. Source-specific physical accounts could show the excess pollution loads at source over the loads corresponding to the standards. The cost of abatement of this excess pollution has to be accounted in the estimation of NNP corrected for urban air pollution.

These two valuation methods provide estimates of cost and benefits of air pollution abatement. However, the cost estimates are for the air pollution at source and the benefits estimates are for the ambient air pollution. Urban air quality modeling establishes the link between the pollution at source and the ambient pollution so that one could compare the cost of air quality improvement to the benefits. A recent study by Sudhakar Yedla et al. (2002) has done urban air quality modeling for the cities of Delhi and Mumbai for finding the relationship between the emissions from different sources and the ambient air quality in the city. This study makes an estimate of reduction of TSPM by 2.37 thousand tonnes from the transport sector in Delhi in comparison to the business-as-usual scenario in the year 2005 due to introduction of CNG in all buses and small cars. This intervention results in a 30 percent reduction in the contribution of the transport sector to the ambient air pollution, measured as TSPM concentration in a cubic meter. An average of the estimates of contribution of the transport sector to the hourly ambient concentration of SPM at seven monitoring stations in Delhi in the business-as usual-scenario works out to be $0.75\mu/m^3$. A 30 percent reduction in this amounts to $0.215\mu/m^3$. Therefore, an estimated reduction in the ambient pollution of TSP in Delhi due to one tonne reduction of TSP at source works out to be mg. $0.00009\mu/m^3$. Estimates described earlier show that a typical household in Delhi is willing to pay ₹ 152 annually for one micro gram reduction of atmospheric concentration of TSPM. Now the household annual willingness to pay for this reduction becomes ₹ 0.014 and extrapolating it to the estimated 23,47,942 urban households in Delhi, the shadow price of a tonne of TSPM becomes ₹ 32,871.

Urban air pollution is an environmental externality created by polluters and therefore the shadow price of air pollution defined above depends upon the size of the exposed population to pollution. For example, a typical urban settlement in India has a population of one million with 2.5 lakh households. It is important to see what is the shadow price of a tonne of TSPM if 2.5 lakh households are exposed to air pollution levels currently found in the mega cities of Delhi, Mumbai, Kolkata, Hyderabad. etc. The studies mentioned above (Murty, Gulati and Banerjee, 2003; Murty and Gulati, 2005) also provide estimates of the household marginal annual willingness to pay for the reduction of one microgram concentration of TSPM in the cities of Kolkata and Hyderabad at ₹ 96.76 and ₹ 220.67 respectively. Given these estimates, the average of household marginal willingness to pay for the reduction of TSPM for the three cities could be computed as ₹ 156.33. The shadow price of one tonne of TSPM in an urban area having one million population in India is estimated at ₹ 3,525.

Conclusion

The current literature on environmental and resource economics provides accounting principles for measuring a country's green GDP. In the case of renewable environmental resources, the cost of sustainable use of the resource has to be accounted for, while for exhaustible resources, the rents for the resource extraction and the cost of avoiding the environmental degradation consequent upon the resource extraction have to be accounted.

There are some recent developments suggesting the generalization of conventional national income accounts and input output accounting methods for estimating green GDP. In both the cases, the approaches suggest the development of natural resource accounts as satellite accounts to the core conventional accounts of measuring GDP.

The case studies of valuation and environmental resource accounting attempted in this paper provide insights into the micro foundations of national income accounts for estimating the green GDP. A case study of the most important air polluting sector—thermal power generation in Andhra Pradesh state—describes possible approaches for measuring the cost of environmentally sustainable development.

The case study of the urban air shed of Delhi describes the approaches of developing natural resource accounts for urban air pollution taking into account damages to households.

End Notes

1. See for details, Samuelson (1961) and Weitzman (1976).
2. Solow (1974); Hartwick (1977, 1978a,b); Christensen (1989); Pearce et al. (1989); Klaasen and Opschoor (1991); Pearce and Turner, (1990) and Daly (1990).
3. Hartwick (1977; 1990); Maler (1991) and Maler and Dasgupta (1998).
4. UN (1993b).
5. European Commission (2006).
6. 200 μ gm/m^3 is the safe WHO and MINAS standard for residential area in India.
7. MINAS: Minimum National Standards for Environmental Pollution in India.

References

Baumol, W.J. and Wallace E. Oates (1994), *The Theory of Environmental Policy,* Cambridge University Press.

Christensen, P.P. (1989), Historical Roots for Ecological Economics-Biophysical Versus Allocative Approache, *Ecological Economics.* Vol. 1, pp. 17-36.

Daly, H. (1990), Commentary: Toward Some Operational Principles of Sustainable Development, *Ecological Economics,* Vol. 2, pp. 1-6.

Dasgupta, P. and K.G. Maler (1998), Decentralisation Schemes, Cost-Benefit Analysis, and Net National Product as Measure of Social Well-being, *The Development Economics Discussion Papers Series No.12, LSE, STICERD.*

European Commission (2006), A New Environmental Accounting Framework Using Externality Data and Input Output Tools for Policy Analysis (EXIOPOL).

Freeman, A.M. (1993*), The Measurement of Environmental and Resource Values: Theory and Methods,* Washington D.C.

Hartwick, J.M. (1977), Inter-generational Equity and the Investing of Rents from Exhaustible Resources, *American Economic Review,* Vol. 66, pp. 972-974.

Hartwick, J.M. *(1978a),* Investing Returns from Depleting Renewable Resources and Inter-generational Equity, *Economics Letters,* Vol. 1, pp. 85-88.

Hartwick, J.M. (1978b), Substitution among Exhaustible Resources and Inter-generational Equity, *Review of Economic Studies,* Vol. 45, pp. 347-354.

Hartwick, J.M. (1990), Natural Resources, National Accounting and Economic Depreciation, *Journal of Public Economics*, Vol. 43, pp. 291-304.

Klassen, G. and H. Opschoor (1991), Economics of Sustainability, *Ecological Economics,* Vol. 4, pp. 83-92.

Maler, K.G. (1991), National Accounts and Environmental Resources, *Environmental and Resource Economics,* Vol. 1, pp. 1-15.

Mitchell, R.C. and R.T. Carson (1989), Using Surveys to Value Public Goods: The Contingent Valuation Method, *Resources for the Future,* Washington D.C.

Murty, M.N. and S.C. Gulati (2005), A Generalized Method of Hedonic Prices: Measuring Benefits From Reduced Urban Air Pollution, *IEG Working Paper Series E/254/06*, Institute of Economic Growth, New Delhi.

Murty, M.N., S.C. Gulati, and A. Banerjee (2003), Hedonic Property Prices and Valuation of Benefits from Reducing Urban Air Pollution in India, *Working Paper No. E/237/2003,* Institute of Economic Growth, Delhi.

Murty, M.N. and Surendar Kumar (2004), *Environmental and Economic Accounting for Industry*, New Delhi, Oxford University Press.

Murty, M.N., Surender Kumar and Kishore K. Dhavala (2006), Measuring Environmental Efficiency of Industry: A Case Study of Thermal Power Generation in India, *IEG Working Paper Series E/270/06*, Institute of Economic Growth, Delhi.

Pearce, D.W. et al. (1989), *Blue Print for a Green Economy,* Earthscan: London.

Pearce, D.W. and R.K. Turner (1990), Economics of Natural Resources and the Environment, Hemel Hemstead-Harvester-Wheatsheaf.

Solow, R.M. (1974), The Economics of Resources or the Resources of Economics, *American Economic Review,* Vol. 64, pp. 1-14.

Sudhakar, Yedla et al. (2002), Air Quality Modeling: Case Studies of Delhi and Mumbai, Indira Gandhi Institute of Development Research, Mumbai.

U.N. (1993), *Integrated Environmental and Economic Accounting*, Interim version (Sales No. E93 XVII; UN 12), New York, United Nations.

Weitzman, M. (1976), On the Welfare Significance of National Product in a Dynamic Economy, *Quarterly Journal of Economics*, Vol. 90, pp. 156-162.

2

Environment, Globalization, Trade and Sustainability

Sarmila Banerjee

Rapid growth of India is a post-liberalization phenomenon where increased openness and global connectivity have been identified as the drivers of growth. The process of liberalization in India was initiated in 1985 and India's participation in world trade has increased steadily since then. The share of trade as a percentage of GDP in India has gone up from 9 percent in 1978-79 to 36 percent in 2008-09 (Figure 2.1).

Figure 2.1: India's Trade Openness: 1978-79 to 2008-09

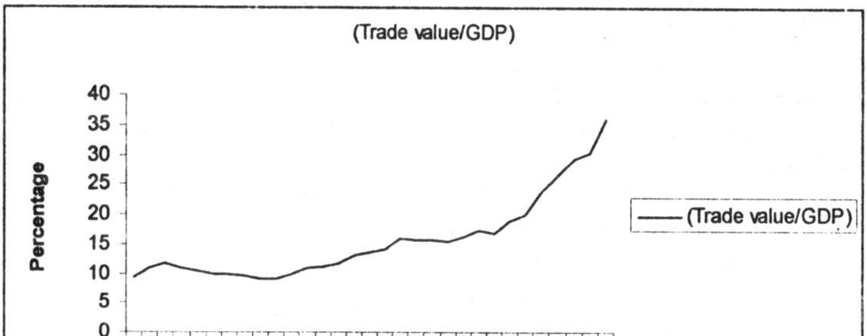

Source: Calculated from data available at www.rbi.org.in.

The effect of trade liberalization on the environment of developing countries is a widely debated topic. Trade enables a country to consume a good without incurring the pollution externality created during its production. So, the importing country effectively displaces the implicit pollution load to the exporting country. With liberalization, the differences in environmental standards between the developed and developing countries might encourage *environmental load displacement* towards the latter. However, the New World Order under the aegis of the WTO recommends implementation of uniform environmental standards in all the member countries and so, since 1995, the process of globalization is also expected to encourage adoption of cleaner production techniques and better abatement practices all over the world. For a country like India, where a large part of production is organized in the informal sector, it is doubtful whether introduction of uniform regulation would lead to adoption of cleaner production techniques in the formal sector or create an escape route to outsource polluting processes to informal sector units and retain the cost competitiveness in the world market. Thus, in the presence of regulatory leakages, trade liberalization might impose significant environmental costs on the economy and make the process of rapid growth unsustainable in the long run.

It is interesting to note that the share of dirty exports [2] in India's total exports is very high and has hovered around 65-70 percent throughout (Figure 2.2), across both pre- and post-liberalization as well as pre- and post-WTO regimes. Since India has experienced commendable export growth in the post-liberalization period, such high share of dirty exports might impose significant environmental costs on the economy unless the WTO norms encourage adoption of cleaner production and abatement techniques. Hence, the moot point is whether the source of this competitive advantage of India in the international market is located in her structural strength or weakness? In case of former, the trade-led growth will be sustainable in the long run but in case of latter, the economic prosperity and environmental sustainability may move in opposite direction.

To examine this position, a number of exercises have been carried out and presented below. We have started with: (a) an analysis of the nature of India's revealed comparative advantage (RCA) in the world market in dirty products followed by, (b) a constant market share (CMS) analysis in dirty products, and (c) the pollution content of India's trade. Finally, (d) a case study of gems and jewelry industry is reported to highlight the nature of possible regulatory leakages and concern for environmental sustainability.

Figure 2.2: Share of Dirty Exports in India's Total Export: 1978-79 to 2008-09

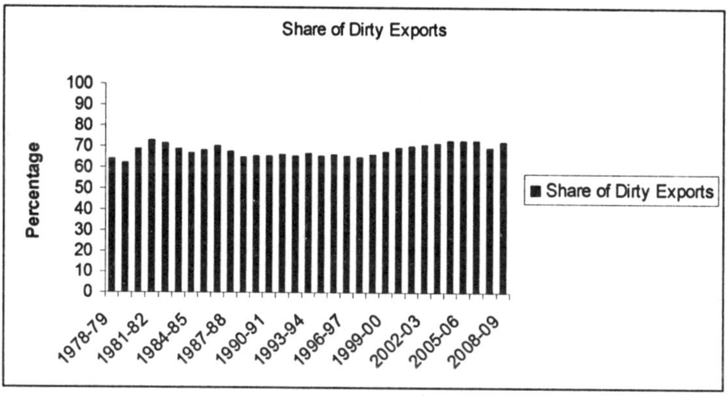

Sources: Calculated from data available at www.rbi.org.in and WITS COMTRADE.

India's Revealed Comparative Advantage in Dirty Products

To assess the change in the pattern of dominance of dirty exports in India's total export after the WTO, the RCA indices of all major dirty commodity groups exported by India have been estimated for two different points of time: 1985-88 representing early liberalization and pre-WTO period and 2005-08 representing matured stage of globalization in post-WTO regime. Major dirty export items have been divided into seven commodity groups: (dirty) primary products, leather, textiles, engineering goods, chemical products, petroleum products and gems and jewelry. For each group, the RCA index has been calculated for each year and for each phase the average values over four years are reported in Table 2.1.

The RCA [3] index is defined as the ratio between the share of a product in total export of a country in relation to the corresponding share of that product in total world export. If the relative country share is greater than the relative world share, i.e., the RCA index is greater than unity, then the country is said to reveal a comparative advantage in that product.

Table 2.1: India's RCA Indices (Dirty Commodity Groups)

Commodity Group	1985-88	2005-08
Dirty Primary Products	1.46	1.10
Leather	13.56	3.29
Textiles	3.22	4.20
Engineering Goods	0.35	0.98
Chemical Products	0.52	1.03
Petroleum Products	1.27	3.30
Gems and Jewelry	15.18	12.53

Source: Calculated on the basis of COMTRADE data (WITS/SITC).

It is interesting to note that during 2005-08, except engineering goods, the RCA values for all dirty commodity groups exceed unity and for the engineering goods also the value has gone up from 0.35 in 1985-88 to 0.98 in 2005-08.

The RCA indices of (dirty) primary products, textile products, engineering goods, chemical products, and petroleum products have shown commendable increase between the pre- and post-WTO period, whereas for leather and gems and jewelry, the high RCA values have been maintained throughout.

Hence, the change in the global economic order does not seem to have any significant impact on the revealed pattern of India's comparative advantage in the world market. This strong presence of dirty products may be due to overall increase in the volume of dirty trade all over the world, change in commodity composition of export basket, change in destination of export or and increase in price competitiveness in the international market. A constant market share analysis would help us to achieve that decomposition.

CMS Analysis of the Change in India's Dirty Exports

A country's export may grow due to four factors: (a) growth of world export; (b) growth of export to relatively faster growing regions; (c) concentration of export in commodities for which demand is growing relatively fast; and (d) more effective competition with other sources of supply. For the first three factors, the export-growth will be experienced even by maintaining a constant market share. However, the fourth factor, if effective, will lead to an increase in the relative market share. CMS analysis can isolate the contribution of first three factors in the observed change in export between two points in time and the residual effect is designated as the change due to price competitiveness. [4] Table 2.2 presents the CMS decomposition for previously selected two sub-periods.

By following the World Bank's TRADECAN 2005 database, the entire world market (where India is an exporter of dirty products) has been divided into eight blocs, viz., North America, Western Europe, other Industrialized Countries, Developing Africa, Central and South America, other Developing America, Developing Asia and others. The dirty goods are sub-divided into the following eight categories where along with the previously reported seven categories, an eighth one has been added as other dirty goods.

The decomposition analysis suggests that the change in the volume of dirty exports from India is not solely due to the increase in the growth of trade in dirty products world-wide; in fact, here the influence has gone down from 89.61 percent to 72.93 percent over the two periods considered here. There is some gain observed due to market diversification (from -12.54 percent to 5.37 percent) but there was very little incentive noted in terms of changing commodity composition (a decline from 11.21 percent to -9.02 percent).

Table 2.2: CMS Analysis of India's Dirty Export Growth

Change in Dirty Export	Change in Absolute Value (million USD): 1985-1988	Percent	Change in Absolute Value (million USD): 2005-2008	Percent
Change in Total Export $V'_{..} - V_{..}$	3461.88	100.00	58555.83	100.00
Increase in World Trade $rV_{..}$	3102.33	89.61	42702.42	72.93
Change in Market Distribution $\sum_j (r_j - r)V_{.j}$	-434.22	-12.54	3145.04	5.37
Change in Commodity Composition $\sum_i \sum_j (r_{ij} - r_j)V_{ij}$	388.15	11.21	-5284.08	-9.02
Change in Competitiveness $\sum_i \sum_j (V'_{ij} - V_{ij} - r_{ij}V_{ij})$	405.63	11.72	17992.44	30.73

Source: Calculated on the basis of COMTRADE data (WITS/SITC).

Hence, India's dirty exports almost stick to their original band, explored a few newer markets and the most important factor influencing her global presence in dirty trade being price competitiveness where it has gone up from 11.72 percent to 30.73 percent. Thus, our CMS analysis suggests that our dirty exports are competitive in the world market and this competitiveness is improving over time. Therefore, in spite of imposition of new regulatory standards in the post-WTO regime, India is managing to retain her competitive cost advantage in the world market.

It is possible that India has managed to retain its competitiveness even after meeting the mandatory compliance obligations in the post-WTO regime by adopting greener technology. If the firms use cleaner production techniques then even when the volume of dirty exports continues to increase, the associated pollution and social costs might not go up. So, it is imperative to check how far the technological improvement may account for this enhanced competitiveness. In fact, production and export of some apparently clean products may also generate excess pollution through input chain. So, instead of concentrating on the dirty products alone it would be wise to estimate the total pollution content of our trade vector and its change over time following changes in the underlying technological set-up indicated by the input-output transaction tables.

Pollution Content of India's Trade

An explicit trade flow has implicit pollution content. The total pollution content of exports and imports can be defined in terms of direct and indirect abatement costs of the exportables vis-à-vis that of the importables. Hence, the pollution content ratio would help us to determine whether in the post-liberalization period, the pattern of pollution load displacement to India from the rest of the world has undergone any significant change. Here, two alternative definitions of pollution content of trade have been used. The first is the total pollution content of trade and the other is the relative pollution content of trade. Total pollution content of trade is defined as the ratio between the total pollution content of exports to the total pollution content of imports. The second one is defined as the ratio of pollution content per rupee of exports to pollution content per rupee of imports.

If $E = (E_1, E_2, \ldots\ldots, E_n)'$ is the export bundle and the corresponding unit abatement cost vector is $C = (C_1, C_2, \ldots C_n)$ then $CE' = \sum_{i=1}^{n} C_i E_i$ will give a measure of the explicit/direct abatement content of the export bundle. Direct abatement content misses out a significant portion of the abatement cost implicit in the production process through the input chain. Hence, to find the total pollution content of the export (or import) bundle, one must also find out the abatement content of the inputs used in producing these final traded goods. This concept can be best captured in terms of inter-industry interdependence formalized in a typical Leontief Static Open Model (LSOM). If there are n sectors in the economy and E is the final export vector that the system wants to support, then $X = AX + E \Rightarrow X = (I - A)^{-1} E$ where $X = (X_1, X_2, \ldots X_n)'$ is the output vector needed to support E and A is the $(n \times n)$ input-output matrix. So, the total pollution content of E will be equal to $\theta = C'X$ *i.e.* $C' (I-A)^{-1} E$ where C is the abatement cost vector representing the abatement costs as percentage of output of the different I-O sectors. Similarly, for import (M) it would be $\delta = C' (I-A)^{-1} M$. So, the pollution content of trade can now be expressed as:

Total pollution content of trade (TPC) = θ/δ

Relative pollution content of trade (RPC) = $(\theta/E)/(\delta/M)$,

The pollution content of India's trade vector has been calculated for six different years, viz., 1985, [5] 1992, 1996, 2000 and 2004 and 2008 (Table 2.3). [6] The year 1985 is chosen as the benchmark. The year 1992 is the year immediately following the official announcement of liberalization whereas the years 1996, 2000, 2004 and 2008 are chosen at four yearly intervals to show the state of pollution trading at a matured stage of globalization following the inception of WTO. To do that, data on the values of export and imports for each of these years, I-O tables for each of these years and the abatement costs of the I-O sectors are required. Annual export import data at SITC 3-digit level categories has been obtained from WITS database COMTRADE. Input-output tables have been taken from the input output transactions tables published by the Central Statistical Organisation (CSO) at an interval of five years. Since the input-output tables for the years under consideration are not available, for finding the pollution content of trade for a particular year, the most recent [7] input-output table published preceding that year has been used. For finding the pollution content of trade in 1985, the commodity x commodity I-O table for 1983-84 has been used. For 1992, the 1989-90 I-O tables have been used, and so on. Finally, for 2004 and 2008, 2003-04 [8] tables have been used. Abatement cost data for the Indian industries for all NIC-87 [9], 3-digit level categories has been obtained from Annual Survey of Industries (ASI) 1997-98, published by the CSO.

Table 2.3: Pollution Content of India's Trade (₹ million)

Symbol	Definition	1985	1992	1996	2000	2004	2008
Θ	PCE	12409	54398	159438	275818	502166	253568.8
Δ	PCM	26519	58470	168908	227800	545811	424222.2
$\left(\theta/\delta\right)$	Total PCR	0.468	0.93	0.944	1.211	0.92	0.60
$\left[\left(\frac{\theta}{E}\right)\Big/\left(\frac{\delta}{M}\right)\right]$	Relative PCR	0.845	1.087	1.084	1.4	1.093	1.02

Sources: Calculated from WITS COMTRADE and CSO database.
Note: PCE: Pollution Content of Export; PCM: Pollution Content of Import; PCR: Pollution Content Ratio.

Starting from 1985 and up to 2000, there was a steady increase in both the total as well as relative pollution content of export. However, a significant turnaround was noted since 2000. In 2004, the ratios were smaller than those of 2000 and in 2008, the declining trends continued. Two possible explanations could be extended—initial increase in the pollution content was the cumulated expression of scale and composition effect; however, with the increase in growth and per capita income, the domestic demand for cleaner environment would go up, leading to the adoption of greener technology and thus, the dominance of the technique effect over the scale and composition ones would lead to a reduction in overall pollution content. Moreover, during this period, the introduction of SPS and TBT agreements might have necessitated introduction of cleaner techniques to adhere to global standards. This technique effect might have led to a fall in the pollution content ratios in the post-2000 period.

Again, the SPS and TBT agreements also made it difficult for developing countries like India to export goods which did not conform to the international environmental standards. As a result, the share of dirty goods in the export basket might have fallen. Thus, along with the technique effect, the composition effect might have also contributed towards a reduction of the pollution content ratios during this period. This explanation loses its credibility once we recall that between 2004 and 2008, there was no scope for observing any technique effect as for both the years the same I-O table has been used to represent technology. Hence, the reduction in pollution content under stringent regulatory regime calls for deeper introspection.

An analysis of the revealed comparative advantage (RCA) indices of all SITC 3-digit level exports for the period 1988-2005 reported in TradeCan 2005 database also reveals that a number of categories identified as dirty [10] by CPCB and belonging to SITC categories 51 (organic chemicals), 53 (dyeing, tanning and colouring materials), 59 (chemical materials and products), 67 (iron and steel) and 69 (manufactures of metal) have shown significant increase in RCAs over the period of analysis. A few other products, whose production process are partly dirty like leather and leather products, gems and jewelry etc. are also showing high RCA. This high RCA values are definitely suggesting some competitive advantages whose nucleolus may be located in improvement in production efficiency or it may be a pseudo-comparative advantage attained through a shifting of pollution load from the formal to the informal sector. For a thorough investigation of these issues, we have taken up a detailed analysis of gems and jewelry industry.

Case Study of Indian Gems and Jewelry Industry

The gems and jewelry industry has witnessed spectacular export growth in the post-liberalization period and has emerged as one of India's leading foreign exchange earners. The question that we would like to address in this paper is whether this competitiveness is based on in-built weaknesses like existence of lax social standards or representing genuine comparative advantage of the industry in the international market.

An analysis of trend, growth and productivity performance of the gems and jewelry sector of India is conducted by using the Annual Survey of Industries (ASI) data between 1984-85 and 2004-05. The entire period has been divided into two sub-periods: 1984-85 to 1994-95 and 1995-96 to 2004-05, where the first sub-period corresponds to pre-reform, pre-WTO situation and the second sub-period represents the post-globalization state. To study the trend we regressed the annual gross value added (Y_t) expressed at 1993-1994 prices, against time (t) and the growth rate is obtained by regressing the natural logarithm of gross value added ($\ln Y_t$) against time (t). The regression coefficients (β's) are representing deterministic time trends and growth rates, respectively. .

The results reported in Table 2.4 indicate an increase in trend value with a decline in growth rate in the later sub-period. To check the hypothesis of structural break, a Chow test has been carried out [11] where the F-value (2.84) turned out to be insignificant at 5 percent level implying a stable structure across the two regimes.

Table 2.4: Trend and Growth of Gems and Jewelry Production: 1984-85 to 2004-05

Equation	Sub-period	B-Coefficient	t-value	p-value	$\overline{R}^2$	df
$Y_t = \alpha + \beta t$	I	2601.00	8.30	0.00	0.87	9
	II	7109.17	2.81	0.02	0.43	8
	I+II	5915.61	9.41	0.00	0.81	19
$\ln Y_t = \alpha + \beta t$	I	0.28	9.20	0.00	0.89	9
	II	0.10	14.53	0.00	0.51	8
	I+II	0.21	14.53	0.00	0.91	19

Source: Calculated from ASI data.

At the next stage, an attempt has been made to verify the evidence of technological progress, if any, over this entire time period. With an implicit assumption of a CRS production technology, the Solow Index [12] helps to decompose this growth of gross value added into the contribution of specific factors (L_t, K_t) as well as that of the total factor productivity A_t. So, $\frac{\Delta Y_t}{Y_t} = \frac{\Delta A_t}{A_t} + w_t \frac{\Delta L_t}{L_t} + r_t \frac{\Delta K_t}{K_t}$ where $\frac{\Delta Y_t}{Y_t}$ = rate of change of gross value added; $\frac{\Delta L_t}{L_t}$ = rate of change of labour force; $\frac{\Delta K_t}{K_t}$ = rate of change of fixed capital; w_t = share of labour in gross value added; r_t = share of capital in gross value added and $\frac{\Delta A_t}{A_t}$ rate of change of total factor productivity.

From the ASI data, information on all variables except A_t can be gathered. L_t is represented by total wages and salaries paid to employees and K_t by gross investment of the year where this gross investment is defined as follows: $I_t = \frac{1}{P_t}[(K_t - K_{t-1}) + D_t]$, where I_t is the gross investment, K_t is the capital stock of period t, D_t is the depreciation and P_t is an appropriate deflator. To estimate K_t, the perpetual inventory method [13] has been used and since the gems and jewelry production is reported in a residual industrial category along with a number of other non-specific products, hence, the GDP deflator is used as the relevant deflator to convert the series in constant prices. The series of A_t values would follow as a residual category.

By Solow index $\frac{\Delta A_t}{A_t} = \frac{\Delta Y_t}{Y_t} - [\ w_t \frac{\Delta L_t}{L_t} + r_t \frac{\Delta K_t}{K_t}\ ]$ and $A_{t+1} = A_t\left[1 + \frac{\Delta A_t}{A_t}\right]$.

If A_t at $t = 0$ is taken as unity, then the series for A_t can be generated numerically. The estimated trend of the A_t series is obtained as: $A_t = \underset{(-9.56^*)}{-0.86} - \underset{(-5.71^*)}{0.04}\, t$, $\overline{R}^2 = 0.67$, $df = 19$;

The trend is negative and statistically significant indicating that there is no sign of temporal improvement in total factor productivity. Thus, the possibility of overall technological up-gradation in the production front is not confirmed by the available data.

Thus, the possibility of overall technological up-gradation in the production front is not confirmed by the available data. Next, to examine whether there has been any significant change in the output-oriented technical efficiency in the sector, we have derived the firm level technical efficiency scores using data envelopment analysis (DEA). [14] The analysis has been done for the years 1989-90, 1993-94, 2000-01 and 2004-05 with unit level ASI data at 5-digit level of disaggregation. We found that there has been an overall decline in the output-oriented technical efficiency of the sector over the period of our study. The relative frequency of the firms with technical efficiency score below 0.5 has steadily increased over time (Figure 2.3). The skewness of the distributions have consistently changed from -1.92 to +1.78 and the median value remains always below mean in more recent years, confirming this concentration at the lower end of the distribution in later period.

Figure 2.3: Stacked Bars of Output-oriented Relative Technical Efficiency Scores

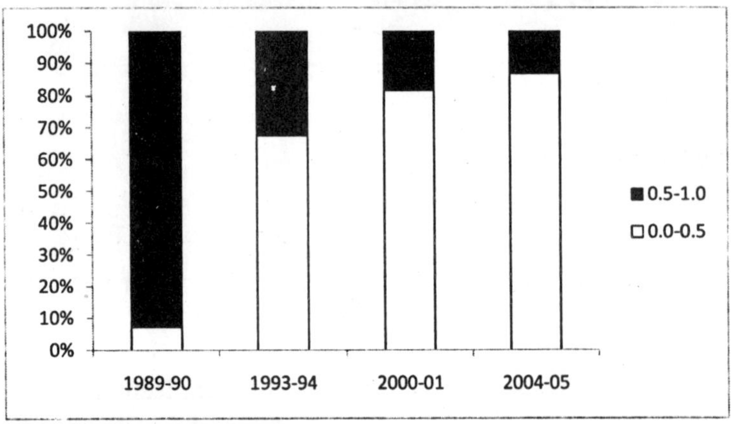

Source: Authors' estimation.

In spite of fabulous export performance, this fall in technical efficiency is indicating an interesting possibility: after reforms, the scope of becoming cost-competitive in the international market has been enhanced for the relatively inefficient new entrants also, who are mostly organizing production through procuring export contracts, importing raw materials and outsourcing the manufacturing process to the informal units to make quick money from the entire transaction. This possibility, if confirmed, will endorse perpetuation of low technical efficiency and the long run sustainability of the recently experienced fortune of the gems and jewelry industry will be questionable. However, the ASI database is not suitable for verifying this line of explanation as here, no export data is reported at the firm level and the information on imported inputs and R&D expenditures are not always adequate. To overcome this limitation, we have utilized the database on listed gems and jewelry making companies consolidated by the Centre for Monitoring Indian Economy (CMIE) in its PROWESS database for the post-reforms period.

Table 2.5: Regression Analysis of Firm-level Performance

Y-Variable	**OUT**	**EXP**
Regression	**1**	**2**
X-Variables	**Fixed Effect**	**Random Effect**
INP	1.033*	0.083
W	-0.773	-1.078
K	0.011	0.270
EXP	1.727***	-
IMP	-2.206**	1.308***
Hausman- χ^2	12.09** (FE)	4.03 (RE)
ρ	0.813	0.418
Wald- χ^2	-	618.76***
BPLM- χ^2	-	9.67***
No. of Groups	20	20
No. of Time Periods	3	3
No. of Observations	60	60

Source: Calculated from CMIE-PROWESS Database.

Twenty listed firms have been identified from the CMIE database on which all relevant information [15] like total output (OUT), total exports (EXP), expenditure on intermediate inputs (INP), expenditure on labour measured in terms of compensation to employees (W), expenditure on capital (K) and import of raw materials (IMR) was available for three selected years, viz., 1996 (to study the early effects of the emergence of WTO on this industry), 2000 (to capture the effects of newer policies like SPS and TBT agreements) and 2005 (when the effect of the new world economic order has been prominently felt on all important transactions).

This helped us to generate a panel of 60 observations. In the regression analysis, OUT and EXP were taken as two dependent variables.

For the regression of OUT (i.e., regression 1), EXP, INP, W, K and IMR were taken as independent variables. In regression 2, the dependent variable was EXP and the independent variables were the different components of cost. The results are reported in Table 2.5.

For all regressions, both fixed effect and random effect models are estimated and on the basis of Hauseman (χ^2) test [16] the appropriate method of estimation has been selected. For OUT, (regression 1), in terms of Hauseman's χ^2 test, the Fixed Effect model has been accepted.

This means there exists reasonable degree of heterogeneity among the constituent firms of the sector in terms of their input-output correspondence and therefore, the firm-specific effects are dominantly present in the system. Here, explanatory variables like INP, IMR and EXP are important factors; however, W and K do not appear to be statistically significant. The performance of OUT has been strongly influenced by EXP. So, at least, a part of the growth of the sector is export-led.

Finally, in the regression of EXP on the different cost components (regression 2) only, IMR turns out to be statistically significant.

Hence, the export performance is neither explained by improved machineries nor by the improved fortune of the workers. Here, the Random Effect model turned out to be the more appropriate one. [17] It seems to indicate that the more export-oriented production unit is importing raw material, outsourcing the follow up processes to the informal sector and re-exporting the finished product.

Since in a putting out system the intermediary firms are tied to the lead firms and organize production strictly according to the guidelines specified by the lead firm, the intermediary firm has little incentive or freedom to experiment and innovate.

This possibility could become the reality provided the production nexus of the sector would reveal close connectivity between formal and informal units. So, we undertook a primary survey on the jewelry-making units of Kolkata in 2008-09 to get insights into the organizational characteristics of the industry. The findings of that survey are reported below.

Primary Survey

We have chosen Kolkata as our area of survey [18] as Kolkata accounts for almost all of the jewelry exports from the eastern region and a large number of both registered and unregistered gems and jewelry producing firms are located here. Kolkata mainly manufactures plain gold and silver jewelry and most of jewelry produced here is crafted in the small informal manufacturing units.

Here, most of the goldsmiths are concentrated in a few localities: Bowbazar and Taltala in Central Kolkata, Garanhata, Sovabazar and Sinthi in North Kolkata and Bhowanipur-Kalighat, Ballygaunge-Dhakuria and Behala in South Kolkata. We have selected the three sites for our field survey; Bowbazar from Central and Garanhata and Sinthi from North. [19]

The initial plan was to collect information on 300 units each, from both Bowbazar and Sinthi and another 200 units from Garanhata. However, though in Bowbazar and Garanhata we managed to conduct the survey as per schedule after facing some initial resistance from the goldsmiths, in Sinthi due to extreme reluctance and active resistance from the goldsmiths information could be collected from 85 units [20] only before abandoning the survey formally.

The salient features of the majority of units surveyed are briefly discussed below.

Inter-linkages between the Formal-Informal Units: A unit to be labeled as a formal unit, must be registered with a number of official bodies and obtain a host of licenses like the trade license, manufacturing license, etc. As Table 2.6 reveals, most of the units surveyed did not have all the required licenses.

Table 2.6: License Status of the Survey Units

Name of the License(s)	No. of Units in Bowbazar (percent)	No. of Units in Garanhata (percent)	No of Units in Sinthi (percent)	Total No. of Units (percent)
NOC	91 (30.2)	51 (25.5)	4 (1.3)	146 (24.9)
Trade License	292 (97.0)	199 (99.5)	83 (99.8)	574 (97.9)
Karigari License	108 (35.8)	47 (23.4)	19 (22.4)	174 (29.7)
Health License	190 (63.1)	104 (52.0)	27 (31.8)	321 (54.8)
NOC + Trade License	90 (29.9)	51 (25.5)	4 (1.3)	145 (24.7)
NOC + Karigari License	31 (10.2)	3 (1.5)	0 (0.0)	34 (5.8)
NOC + Trade + Karigari+Health	30 (10.0)	3 (1.5)	0 (0.0)	33 (5.6)
Total	301 (100)	200 (100)	85 (100)	586 (100)

Source: Primary Survey.

It is interesting to note that that out of the 586 units, 130 do not have any license at all (Table 2.6).

Hence, these 130 are purely informal unregistered units. In fact only 33 manufacturing units claimed to have all kinds of licenses, and, therefore, formal in nature.

Since the jewelry making process is divided into a number of operations viz. refining, crafting or making of jewelry, finishing (which includes polishing) and Galai or recycling, each demanding some specialized craftsmanship, most of the units surveyed concentrate in a sub-group of operations.

Out of 586 units surveyed, 58.2 percent were specializing in any particular stage of production (refining, making, finishing or recycling) and the rest were involved in more than one stage.

However, only 4 percent were carrying out the entire process *from cradle to grave* under the same roof. The small informal units get manufacturing orders from the large (registered) jewelry shops on the basis of a putting out type contract.

The formal sector firms procure orders, organize production through sub-contracting chains and also take care of the marketing and related promotional activities. Thus, the small units are interconnected with one another and the larger firms through a long sub-contracting chain.

Lack of Environmental Compliance: The solid waste from these units consists of traces of acid, iron particles etc. and the liquid waste consists of acid water. The gaseous wastes consist mainly of the acid and cadmium fumes emitted during production.

Of the 586 units covered in our survey, not a single one had any provision to treat waste. 434 units (i.e. 74.06 percent) admitted that they dump their liquid wastes [21] in the municipal drain and 508 units (86.69 percent) admitted that they sell the sediment from the liquid waste to the *Niharawalas* [22] (Table 2.7).

To check air pollution, the WBPCB has designed special equipment fitted with special scrubbers to absorb the toxic acid fumes. However, not a single unit used the equipment. Another source of pollution in gold manufacturing emanates from the use of cadmium as soldering agent.

In our survey, we found that about 98 percent of the firms involved in crafting of jewelry, use cadmium even though cadmium fumes are extremely toxic and both the World Gold Council and Bureau of Indian Standards forbids its use.

Thus, environmental laws are routinely flouted by the informal units exposing the surrounding population and the goldsmiths to serious health hazards.

Out of 586 units surveyed, 451 (i.e. about 76.96 percent) units reported that they would have to shut down if they were forced to follow the pollution control norms.

Table 2.7: Mode of Disposal of Liquid Waste

Mode of Liquid Waste Disposal	No. of Units in Bowbazar	No. of Units in Garanhata	No. of Units in Sinthi	Total No. of Units
Niharawala	271	168	69	508
Drain	227	158	49	434
Niharawala+Drain	204	131	34	369
None reported	7	5	1	13

Source: Primary Survey.

Absence of Social Security Provisions: The goldsmiths earn a paltry sum of money and are exposed to serious pollution in return of their hard work and exquisite artistic talent which enables the formal sector jewelry firms and the exporters to reap huge profits.

They are also denied the benefits of statutory provident fund and employees' state insurance schemes.

No Up-gradation of Physical and Human Capital: None of the firms reported to have made any investment in infrastructure development in the last ten years.

Our primary survey on gems and jewelry sector indicates that the production structure is characterized by extensive inter-linkage between the formal and informal sector and in most of the manufacturing units, the features of a subsistence sector like low wage, poor working conditions and lack of concern for worker safety and environmental protection is present.

This inter-connectedness is suggestive of an escape route for the formal sector in face of pressure for compliance to environmental and social norms from both national as well as supra-national organizations to retain competitiveness in the world market.

Concluding Observations

At the initial stage of liberalization, developing countries with weaker environmental and social standards might specialize in dirty goods leading to a migration of pollution. As the process of globalization matures, the countries are forced to conform to the global environmental and social norms.

However, the possibility of shifting pollution loads from formal to informal units within a developed country to retain cost competitiveness in the global market cannot be ignored. We have taken up the case of gems and jewelry industry of India to validate this claim.

It appears that the root of competitive advantage of our leading export sectors may be located in the structural weakness of the economy and, if so, the recently experienced high growth may not be sustainable in the long run.

Hence, to ensure sustainable long run growth in a globally integrated world, the policy planners need to pay more attention to address the bottlenecks imposed by the inherent features of underdevelopment by designing suitable instruments for intervention.

End Notes

1. This paper heavily draws from the works conducted jointly with Sudeshna Chattopadhyay of Bidhannagar College, Kolkata. Two articles especially used here are: (i) Chattopadhyay, Sudeshna and Sarmila Banerjee (2012): Shifting of Pollution Loads to Informal Units in India: A Possible Escape Route for Compliance with WTO Standards, *Foreign Trade Review*, Volume 48, No. 1, Sage, and (ii) Chattopadhyay Sudeshna and Sarmila Banerjee (2013): Indian Gems and Jewelry Industry: An Enquiry into the Nature of Competitive Advantage in Sarmila Banerjee and Anjan Chakrabarti (eds.) Development and Sustainability: India in a Global Perspective, Springer.com.
2. Dirty commodities among India's major export items were identified as those classified as Red and Orange category dirty industries by the Central Pollution Control Board (CPCB) and accepted by the Central Statistical Organization (CSO) of India to identify dirty production in manufacturing sector (Chaudhuri and Ray, 2000).
3. $$RCA_{ij} = \frac{x_{ij}/X_j}{x_{iw}/X_w}$$

where x_{ij} = India's export of ith commodity, X_j = India's total export, x_{iw} = World's export of ith commodity; X_w = Total World exports. RCA>1 indicates a revealed comparative advantage.

4. The formulae for CMS decomposition may be developed with the help of the following notations:

$V..$: Value of total dirty exports of India in the base year;

V_{ij}: Value of export of the ith component of dirty export to the jth country by India in the base year;

(The notations with *prime* ['] represent corresponding final year figures).

r: Percentage increase of total world export of dirty commodities from the base year to the final year;

r_j: Percentage increase of total world export of dirty commodities to country j from the base year to the final year;

r_i: Percentage increase of world export of ith component of dirty commodity export from the base year to the final year;

r_{ij}: Percentage increase of world export of the ith dirty component to country j from the base year to the final year;

Therefore, $V_{..} = \sum_j V_{.j} = \sum_i V_{i.} = \sum_i \sum_j V_{ij}$; ....(A)

The change in export over two different points in time is given by: $V'_{..} - V_{..}$;

At the first level this can be expressed as:

$V'_{..} - V_{..} = rV_{..} + \left(V'_{..} - V_{..} - rV_{..}\right)$, where the first term in the RHS isolates the effect of change in world export and the second term is the residual effect of competitiveness. At the second level the effect of change in the direction of trade can be isolated by using relation (A) as follows:

$$\sum_j V'_{.j} - \sum_j V_{.j} = rV_{..} + \sum_j (r_j - r)V_{.j} + \sum_j \left(V'_{.j} - V_{.j} - r_j V_{.j}\right),$$

where the second term in the RHS represents the effect of change in the value of export due to change in the direction of trade, and the first and third terms carry their usual meaning. Finally, at the third level, by using relation (A), the effect of change in the commodity composition can be isolated as follows:

$$\sum_i \sum_j V'_{ij} - \sum_i \sum_j V_{ij} = rV_{..} + \sum_j (r_j - r)V_{.j} + \sum_i \sum_j (r_{ij} - r_j)V_{ij} + \sum_i \sum_j \left(V'_{ij} - V_{ij} - r_{ij}V_{ij}\right),$$

.... (B)

Here, the third term on the RHS is representing the contribution of change in the commodity composition to the change in dirty export, and the other terms carry their usual meaning.

5. The year 1985 refers to financial year 1985-86, 1992 refers to the financial year 1992-93 and so on.
6. In the thesis, we have calculated Pollution Content till 2004.
7. The implicit assumption is that in the intermediate period between the publications of the two input-output tables the technology remains constant.
8. Input-output tables after 2003-04 has not yet been published by

the CSO. Hence, we had to use 2003-04 tables for 2008.

9. The abatement cost for any I-O category is derived as the weighted average of the abatement costs of the constituent SITC categories, with the relative trade share in value terms as relevant weights. The calculation involves extensive matching of input-output categories with SITC categories and NIC categories. The details of the methodology have been discussed in detail in the thesis.
10. The commodities identified as dirty in our study are those that have been classified as orange or red category dirty industries by the Central Pollution Control Board (CPCB) and the Central Statistical Organization (CSO) of India.
11. $F = \left\{ {[RSS_p - (RSS_1 + RSS_2)]/k} \Big/ {[(RSS_1 + RSS_2)/(n-k)} \right\}$

$\sim F_{k,(n-k)}$, and $F_{(2,17)},_{.05} = 19.4$

12. Growth accounting approach.
13. K_t is obtained by the perpetual inventory method as follows:

$K_t = K_0 + \sum_{i=1}^{t-1} I_{t-i}$ where K_o is the capital stock in the benchmark year. Here, we have selected 1973-74 as the benchmark year and 1993-94 as the reference period for GDP-deflator.

14. Roy (2003) and Coelli (1998) present comprehensive discussion of DEA technique.
15. We found that expenditure on R&D is extremely low and very few firms reported any expenditure on R&D during the years under consideration. Hence, it is apparent that R&D has not exercised any significant influence on the performance of the sector. So, R&D has not been included as an explanatory variable in our regression analysis.
16. With Random Effect as the Null Hypothesis.
17. It is likely that the exporting firms function in a putting out system and work as a part of global production chain where the main function of these exporting intermediary firms is to import raw materials, get the production stages done by the informal sector units and re-export the finished product. For example, the diamond processing firms import rough diamonds and after

processing re-export the processed diamonds. In fact, 85 percent of the world's diamonds are processed in India and the diamond cutting firms in India has strong production links with the leading diamond retailers and manufacturers like De Beers, Alrosa, BHP Billiton;
(www.afdiamonds.com; http://catchef.ft.com).

18. The primary survey has been conducted as a part of the research project titled, "Environmental Regulation and Process Sub-Contracting: A Study of Gems and Jewellery Manufacturing Units in Kolkata", UGC Sanction No: PWH 007/06-07(ERO) sponsored by the University Grants Commission (UGC) under the UGC Minor Research Project scheme.
19. No unit from South-zone has been surveyed as we had to abandon the survey abruptly because of active resistance from the local gold traders' associations.
20. The reluctance of the goldsmiths to face the interviewers might be due to the fact that most of the units did not have the necessary licenses and did not follow the laws especially those related to labour and environmental standards. The goldsmiths were apprehensive that due to increased public attention through media coverage they might be subjected to serious regulatory monitoring. The resistance from the goldsmiths was so hostile that we were forced to abandon our survey after interviewing only 85 units there. Sinthi is reportedly infamous for clandestine cross border trade in gold. This might be the reason why we had to face extraordinarily active resistance from the goldsmiths.
21. A survey conducted by Kolkata Metropolitan Development Authority (KMDA) back in 1999 in the advent of setting up of Manikanchan SEZ in Kolkata revealed that the liquid waste, especially the acid from gold manufacturing which is being disposed through Kolkata Municipal Corporation (KMC) drain in huge quantities without any processing is slowly seeping through and is getting mixed with underground water to become a source of health hazard (see KMDA, February 2003).
22. The *Niharawalas* are a class of people who earn their living by extracting gold from the wastes that they buy from jewelry manufacturing units The *Niharawalas* do not possess any kind of license and extract gold from the wastes through a very polluting process. After extracting the gold from the residues,

they dump the remaining solid waste in open and the liquid in public drains.

3

Green Outcomes of Rural Development Programmes in India

P.P. Mitra, N.K. Sahu, Mahipal and Mukesh Kumar

The efficacy of rural development programmes, apart from poverty alleviation among others, is also measured by the green outcomes of such programmes since the issue of sustainable development has become paramount in the development agenda. In this paper we will examine the issues connected with measuring green outcomes given the fact that the methodology to measure such outcomes is quite complex and may not be easy to implement at the practical level.

Theoretical Formulations of Green Outcomes

Procedures for estimating the valuation as the accounting prices of goods and services began in the World Bank in 1970s (Squire and vander Taak, 1975). The theory of accounting prices that existed at that time assumed that the social cost-benefit analysis was applied in a framework where an optimal economic policy was in place (Little and Mirrlees, 1974). In contrast, (Dasgupta, Marglin and Sen, 1972) assumed that policy reforms would have to be made in an economy beset with inefficiencies and inequalities.

A significant weakness in the earlier framework was the lack of the environmental dimension. The realisation to introduce such a green dimension became clear from market failures since markets did not exist for many natural resources and the services they supported (Dasgupta et al., 2011). The interaction between biodiversity, ecological functioning, eco-system services and the production of goods are not signalled by market prices and thereby came the need to find avenues to incorporate green computations in measuring outcomes of economic decision-making and its evaluation. A good deal of work has, however, gone into environmental and resource economics to estimate the accounting prices of environmental resources (Mitchell and Carson, 1989; Freeman, 1992; and Dasgupta and Maler, 2000). It was increasingly realised that estimates of GNP and commonly used socio-economic indicators as GNP per capita could be misleading since they often did not take into consideration resource degradations, making activities unsustainable.

It also began to be realized that many transactions take place in non-market institutions involving environmental services. Some theoretical and empirical literature has developed in this area. For instance, (Ostrom, 1996) in her work on collectively managed irrigation systems in Nepal attempted to account for differences in rights and responsibilities among users. These users are often not homogeneous with some receiving water as head-enders while others could be tail-enders. The distribution is often not equitable among them with the head-enders receiving more as compared to the tail-enders. In the Indian context, Chopra and Dasgupta (1992) have worked on common pool resources wherein they have underlined the need to estimate such resources and designing interventions to focus on processes that internalise the perception of stake holders in resource ownership.

In the economic literature, the linkage between welfare economics theory and green national accounts has been extensively studied (Dasgupta, 2008). He goes on to show that GNP's main weakness is the fact that it does not take into consideration the depreciation of capital assets which the concept of NNP does, which lays down the ceiling to be imposed on aggregate consumption if the economy's wealth is not to decline. This argument has been advanced by Lindahl (1933) and further elaborated by Solow (1974), Hartwick

(1977) and Dixit et al. (1980). The concept of depreciation is particularly significant in our discussion since natural resources are subject to considerable depreciation ranging from 100 percent of the services drawn from oil and natural gas which are non-renewable to the depreciation experienced by the mismanagement of eco-systems. It is, therefore, very important that these depreciations be accounted for in the national income accounts. In a much noted paper, Weitzman (1976) showed that NNP measured in shadow prices is proportional to inter-generational well-being and proves that the present value of current NNP (held constant) is just equal to the present value of consumption along the optimal growth path of the economy.

This proposition has, however, been challenged by Dasgupta (2008), who states that well-being is not the same as consumption. Dasgupta (2008) further criticizes the theoretical formulations as most of the models assume: (i) economics at a full welfare optimum, (ii) population constant, (iii) no exogenous technological change, (iv) goods and services have markets and the market prices are the shadow prices, and (v) commodity transformation possibilities are convex which often is not the case and non-linearties are the rule in many of nature's processes.

The approach which does not take into consideration many of the above mentioned restrictive assumptions has been developed by Dasgupta and Maler (2000) and Arrow et al. (2003) which based the welfare economics of green national accounts on economic forecasts. The forecasts assume that cconomy faces not only technological and ecological constraints but also institutional constraints (sometimes called transaction and information constraints) apart from constraints of market structure, structure of property rights, tax rates, non-market institutions of credit, insurance and common property resources. In such a structure, shadow prices equal market prices in those competitive market economies where the set of taxes and subsidies that are required to support an optimum growth path are in place. In imperfect economies, however, market prices are a good substitute for shadow prices only in very limited cases (Little and Mirrlees, 1969, 1974; Dasgupta et al., 1974).

Environmental natural resources are among the many goods and services where market prices do not approximate for shadow prices. Freeman (1993), has studied ways to estimate shadow prices of environmental amenities but the literature on ways to estimate shadow prices of eco-system services remain small. A recent suggestion by Miller et al. (2007) is that the eco-system's resilience, which in the present context is the distance between N (the economy's natural stock) and the nature's threshold should be regarded as a capital asset, which is an important practical consideration towards creation of a system of national accounts that accommodates nature's non-linearties seriously.

Pearce and Atkinson (1993), Hamilton (1994), Pearce et al. (1996) and Serageldin (1995) argued that wealth is the appropriate index to see if economic development is sustainable, but a rigorous proof by Hamilton and Clemnes (1999) and Dasgupta and Maler (2000) suggest that the correct linear index of well-being is not NNP (flow concept) but comprehensive wealth (stock concept) at constant shadow prices. Comprehensive wealth in the literature has been defined as the shadow value of the stocks of the economy's (comprehensive) list of capital assets.

Our review of the theoretical literature suggests that the computation of shadow prices is central to the estimation of green outcomes—as such prices attempt to provide a valuation of assets which are ecologically fragile in a situation where natural resources are scarce and non-renewable. Shadow prices capture the degree of substitution across different forms of capital, contribution to inter-generational well-being at each point of time by each capital asset and also captures expected future scarcities.

Measurable Indicators of Green Outcomes

With the just discussed theoretical perspective in view, in this section we shall examine the applicability, in terms of data availability at the global and regional levels, of measuring sustainable development in terms of wealth. Here, wealth is defined as the social value of the stock of a comprehensive list of capital assets, where the value is measured in terms of shadow prices. Arrow et al. (2003) developed the inclusive wealth framework in which natural capital is defined as everything in nature (biotic and abiotic) capable of contributing to human welfare, either through the production process or directly.

Within the wealth accounting framework, natural capital is defined as the sum of the worth of all natural assets in a given country (Arrow et al., 2010). Accordingly, the First Inclusive Wealth Report (IWR) 2012 brought out jointly by UNEP and UNU-IHDP (United Nations University's International Human Dimensions Programme) is an attempt to carry forward the message of Millennium Ecosystem Assessment of 2005 and the Report of the Stiglitz-Sen-Fitoussi Commission (2010) which argued that well-being would be measured only by a shift from conventional production indicators to those that incorporate non-economic, market-based aspects of well-being, including sustainability issues.

We shall restrict our discussion to the use and conservation of water since water conservation is an important objective of many rural development programmes. The approach to water in the IWR is that evaluation of the natural resource must proceed in two discrete steps: first, the construction of physical water accounts, designed to estimate the amount of water which is present and available, how accessible it is and with what reliability, and second, when the accounts have been finalized, a value needs to be placed for these resources. The UN's System of Environmental Economic Accounting for Water (SEEAW) is an important step towards understanding the flows and stocks of water. The SEEAW distinguishes between consumptive and non-consumptive uses of water. Botswana is a country where there is some progress in water accounting. A typical water accounts report of ground and surface water recharge would look as follows (Tables 3.1 and 3.2).

Table 3.1: Aggregate Accounts

(To be separately computed for ground and surface water)

Items	Year 1	Year 2	Year 3
(I) (a) Opening volume (individual borewell/ pond/percolation/tank/check dams) (b) Abstraction (-) (total volume of water withdrawn in a given year) (c) Recharge (+) (d) Other changes to volume of reserves (+/-) (e) Closing volume (II) (a) Opening volume (Total ground water in the village or area) (b) Abstraction (-) (c) Recharge (+) (d) Other changes to volume of reserves (+/-) (e) Closing volume (III) (a) Opening Volume (total developed ground water in the region/ country) (b) Abstraction (-) (c) Recharge () +) (d) Other changes to volume of resources (+/-) (e) Closing Balance			

Table 3.2: Subsidiary Accounts

(To be separately computed for ground and surface water)

Items	Year 1	Year 2	Year 3
Recharge due to agriculture by reducing abstraction;			
Recharge due to construction by reducing abstraction;			
Recharge due to manufacturing by reducing abstraction;			
Recharge due to reduced use by government sector;			
Recharge due to reduced domestic use.			

Water accounting uses a water balance approach to quantify the amount of water entering a system (borewell, pond, river etc.), either through recharge or through precipitation and the amount leaving the system through evaporation or abstraction. The amounts depleted within the system are then classified according to use. Once water is classified according to use, water accounting indicators help us to refine the policies through estimates of: (a) depleted fraction (amount of water depleted divided by gross inflow), (b) beneficial utilization (amount of water depleted by all beneficial processes to the amount of water available for use), and (c) productivity of water quantified by the value derived from the water used. In agriculture, it can be expressed as the yield per hectare of water consumed by crops. More generally, it can be expressed as the economic value of production per unit of water consumed.

The question now arises as to how the accounting prices or the shadow prices are to be computed to evaluate the socio-economic worth of natural assets. By definition, accounting or shadow prices are measures of the social opportunity cost of resource. The accounting price of a resource is the increase in social well-being that would be enjoyed if a unit more of the resource was made available at no cost (Dasgupta, 2011). In the literature, accounting prices have been seen as the difference between the market price and the tax (or subsidy) that ought to be imposed. Needless to say, accounting prices reflect social objectives, ecological and technological constraints and the extent to which resources are available. As an illustration, in a free economy, if natural resources are given free access, the market price would be zero but being in limited supply the accounting prices would be positive. A policy prescription to improve matters would be to impose regulations as resource users, or impose a tax (often called in the literature as Pigouvian tax, 1920). The idea underlying Pigouvian tax is to bring market prices in line with the accounting prices.

In our illustration of water accounts, we get an idea about the status of the resource availability and its use. Since water is a scarce commodity, society has begun to realize that it cannot be priced at zero and therefore it enjoys a positive accounting price or shadow price. The accounting price could be measured in terms of the public resources generated to construct or maintain water works be it borewells, tanks, ponds and also the associated activities required for desilting, soil conservation, water harvesting etc. Public resources come out of tax payers money and therefore the amount spent from public exchequer per unit of water conserved, recharged or harvested out of such measures could be an approximate estimate of accounting prices or the shadow prices.

Green Outcomes in Rural Development Programmes

We would in this section show the importance of water in some of the rural development programmes. The Mahatma Gandhi National Rural Guarantee Act (MGNREGA), 2005 was legislated with the important objective of generating 100 days of guaranteed wage employment in a financial year to every rural household whose adult members volunteer to do unskilled work. Ensuring livelihood security, among others, improved water security is an important mandate of the Act.

Table 3.3 gives the list of key environmental services associated with MGNREGA.

Table 3.3: MGNREGA and Key Environmental Services

MGNREGA Activities (1)	Local Environmental Services (2)	Regional and Global Environmental Services (3)
Water Conservation and Harvesting	Ground water recharge, soil moisture retention and production (erosion control) flood control (reduced risk); Providing irrigation and drinking water and improving soil quality (nutrient cycling)	Water conservation
Irrigation Provisioning and Improvement	Providing irrigation, improved agriculture and livelihoods, increased crop production	Reduce the need for methane producing large dams
Renovation of Traditional Water Bodies	Improved storage capacity, irrigation availability, ground water recharge, soil quality (nutrient cycling) biomass production and crop production	Water conservation
Drought Proofing	Soil moisture retention, protection (erosion control) and soil quality (nutrient cycling), flood control (reduced risk), bio-mass production (fuel wood) and local climate	Water conservation, carbon sequestration, bio-diversity conservation

	regulation	
Flood Control	Better drainage, higher land productivity (erosion control) and flood control (reduced risk)	Water conservation

Source: MGNREGA *Sameeksha*, Ministry of Rural Development, 2012, p. 39.

Studies found that most assets created under MGNREGA are used for multiple purposes. In the states of Bihar, Rajasthan, Gujarat, Kerala and Madhya Pradesh, almost 50 percent of the assets surveyed were designed for single use such as irrigation. But there were *de facto* multiple structures being used for household purposes, e.g. ground water recharge, livestock, etc. thereby enhancing the water and livelihood security in the village ecosystem. For assessing the development impact of MGNREGA assets, it is necessary to take into account the nature and multi-utility of each asset. The methodology to measure green outcomes is likely to be useful in making a fuller assessment of the multi-utility of each asset, on improving the water conservation and water use through an accounting procedure and also arriving at an estimate of accounting price or the shadow price of water, which is an important natural resource.

Another important rural development programme focused on water conservation is the Integrated Watershed Management Programme (IWMP).

The methodology to measure green outcomes discussed earlier would be useful not only in deriving a water accounting table of the watershed projects but also in assessing the productivity of water.

Policy Implications

The paper attempts to show that the importance of water as a natural resource can only be realised if a proper system of accounting natural resources is put in place. Rural development programmes that have conservation of water as their central focus need to incorporate a system of water accounting so that the impact of these programmes is assessed in a systematic manner. Any evaluation tool or technique that does not take into consideration a system of natural resource accounting to measure the outcome of rural development programmes will remain incomplete. A considerable distance still remains to be travelled to institute a practical system of natural resource accounting in rural development programmes. Nonetheless, attempts need to be made in this direction and the paper has attempted to provide a preliminary approach taking into consideration the example of water, which is an important natural resource, although renewable, but is subject to the vagaries of monsoon.

According to a Mckinsey Report of 2009, water is becoming scarce and water stress is projected to increase with water supply satisfying only 60 percent of world demand in 20 years. To begin with, the evaluation mechanism for all rural development programmes will have to incorporate a fairly detailed reporting format to capture the information that goes towards valuating natural resources. As the next step, the estimation of accounting prices or shadow prices may be facilitated to appreciate the value of natural resources and the efficacy of the rural development programmes in conserving natural resources and bringing about a sustainable development process would need to be understood in this perspective. At a national level, certain action indicators and outcome indicators could be thought about to build the element of natural resource accounting in the policy framework. These arc given in Table 3.4.

The Report of the Twelfth Plan Working Group on Natural Resource Management and Rain-Fed Farming has expressed concern about widespread, serious and continuing degradation of India's natural resource base, which is impacting growth rates in agriculture. The Report strongly argues that sustainable and inclusive growth is not possible unless the processes contributing to resource degradation and vulnerability of rain-fed agriculture and production systems are squarely addressed and redressed. As a first step, it is necessary that a system of water accounting is put in place for all rural development programmes which have water conservation as one of their major focus. It is only then that an objective assessment could be made about the green outcomes of such programmes.

Table 3.4: Action Indicators and Outcome Indicators

Action Indicators	Outcome Indicators
Number of enacted and implemented policy measures and officially approved plans that promote sustainable rural development through better utilization of natural resources	Percentage and amount of land or projects under different rural development programmes which aim at better utilization of natural resources
Level of support to encourage State governments/panchayats to invest in conversion to green rural development measured in terms of conservation and better utilization of water	Increase in water productivity, decline in use of agro-chemicals, increase in the use of bio pesticides
Percentage of rural development budget that is earmarked by central and State Governments for environmental objectives	Increasing proportion of payments for environmental services as a percentage of total budget
Linking release of funds to rural development projects that incorporate natural resource accounting	Increasing proportion of releases for such projects and incentives to states for incorporating such accounting practices

Note: Some of the indicators have been adopted from *Towards a Green Economy*, UNEP, 2011.

The views in the paper are of the authors and the usual disclaimers apply.

References

Arrow, K.J., P. Dasgupta, K.G. Maler (2003a), Evaluating Projects and Assessing Sustainable Development in Imperfect Economies, *Environ Resource Econ*, 26(4), pp. 647-685.

Arrow, K.J., P. Dasgupta, K.G. Maler (2003b), The Genuine Saving Criterion and the Value of Population, *Economic Theory*, 21(2), pp. 217-225.

Arrow, K.J., P. Dasgupta, L.J. Goulder, K.J. Mumford and K. Oleson (2010), Sustainability and the Measurement of Wealth, NBER Working Paper No. 16599.

Chopra, K. and P. Dasgupta (2002), Common Pool Resources in India: Evidence, Significance and New Management Initiatives (Mimeo).

Dasgupta, P., (2008), The Welfare Economic Theory of Green National Accounts, Springer Science Business Media.

Dasgupta, P., A. Kinzig and Charles Perrings (2011), The Value of Biodiversity, October, (Mimeo).

Dasgupta. P, and K.G. Mailer (2000), Net National Product, wealth and social well-being (Environ Dev Eco 5(1), 69-93

Dasgupta, P., S. Marglin and A. Sen (1972), Guidelines for Project Evolution, United Nations, New York.

Dixit, A., P.J Hammond, M. Hoel (1980), On Hartwick's Rule for Regular Maximum Paths of Capital Accumulation and Resources Repletion, *Review of Economic Studies*, 47(3), pp. 551-556.

Freeman, A.M. (1993), The Measurement of Environmental and Resource Value: Theory and Methods, *Resource Future*, Washington D.C.

From *Hariyali* to *Neeranchal*: Report of the Technical Committee on Watershed Programmes in India, Department of Land Resources, Ministry of Rural Development, Government of India, January 2006.

Hamilton, K. and M. Cllemens (1999), Genetic Savings Rates in Developing Countries, World Bank, *Economic Review*, 13(2), pp. 333-356.

Hartwick, J., (1977), International Equity and the Investing of Rents from Exhaustible Resources, *American Economic Review*, 66, pp. 972-974.

Lindahal, E. (1934), The Concept of Income, in G. Bagge (ed.), Economic Essays in Honour of Gustaf Cassel, George Allen and Unwin, London.

Little, I.M.D. and J.A. Mirrlees (1974), Project Appraisal and Planning for Developing Countries, George Allen and Unwin, London.

Millennium Ecosystem Assessment (2005), Ecosystem and Human Well-being: Syntheses, Island Press, Washington D.C.

Miller, K., C.Z. Li and G. Destouni (2007), Pricing Resilience in a Dynamic Environmental System: A Capital Theoretic Approach, Discussion Paper No. 209, Beijer Institute of Ecological Economics, Stockholm.

Mitchell, R.C. and R.T. Carson, (1989), Using Savings to Value Public Goods: The Contingent Valuation Method, Resources for the Future, Washington D.C.

Ostrom, E. (1996), Incentive, Rules of the Game and Development, Proceedings of the Annual World Bank Conference on Development Economics (1955), (Supplement to the World Bank Economic Review and the World Bank Research Observer), pp. 207-234.

Pearce, D. and G. Atkinson (1993), Capital Theory and the Measurement of Sustainable Development: An Indicator of Weak Sustainability, *Ecological Economics*, 8(2), pp. 103-108.

Pigeon, A.C. (1920), The Economics of Welfare, Macmillan & Co., London.

Serageldin, I. (1995), As We Saving Enough for the Future? in Monitoring Environmental Progress, Report on Progress in Environmental Sustainable Development, World Bank, Washington D.C.

Solow, R.M. (1974), International Equity and Exhaustible Resources, *Review of Economic Studies*, 41, (Symposium Issue), pp. 29-45.

Stiglutz, J., A. Sen and J.P. Fitousy (2010), Measuring Our Lives: Why GDP Does Not Add Up, The New Press, New York.

Water Accounts of Botswana (1992-2003), Prepared by the Department of Environmental Affairs in association with the Centre for Applied Research, July 2006.

Glossary

Accounting Prices: Accounting prices or shadow prices are measures of the social opportunity cost of resource use. The accounting price of a resource is the increase in social well-being that would be enjoyed if a unit more of the resources was made available at no cost.

Ecological Functions: The combinations of the eco-system component and ecosystem processes that enable eco-systems to support primary production and to maintain populations of species.

Eco-system Services: The benefits (i.e. goods and services) people obtain from eco-systems.

Eco-system Processes: Biochemical cycling, including primary production (Photosynthesis) nutrient and water cycling, materials decomposition, flow, storage and transformation of materials and energy through an eco-system including through food web processes such as pollution, predation and parasitism.

Social Discount Rates: The rate at which society is willing to substitute future consumption for present consumption.

4

Sodic Reclamation and Economic Sustainability

Sanatan Nayak

Introduction

Large numbers of studies in 1980s and 1990s have identified the negative impact of irrigation induced sodicity in different parts of the country. It reduced productivity, intensity of various crops and made these areas out of cultivation (Joshi and Agnihotri, 1984; Abrol, 1984; Joshi, 1987; Chopra, 1989; Joshi et al., 1992; Dinakar, 1993; Datta et al., 2000; Nayak, 2002). Due to continuous decline of productivity of various crops, the investment made on resource use for cultivation has been declined (Joshi and Agnihotri, 1984; Repetto, 1986; Joshi, 1987; Datta et al., 2000). This further caused the decline in profitability and income of the farming class depending on these affected lands (Joshi et al., 1992; Datta et al., 2000). The eventual impact became severe with the decline of the cultivated land in the canal command areas (Joshi, 1987; Chopra, 1989; Datta et al., 2000). It has led to economic and social instability due to intensive dependence on degraded land (Dinakar, 1993).

Reclamation of degraded land has a long history in Uttar Pradesh. The State government has undertaken various measures for reclaiming degraded land even before the plan era. In 1884, nearly 1,200 hectares of ravine lands were forested by the then collector of Etawah (Dhar, 2004). In 1870, the Reh Committee suggested deepening of canals for reducing saline efflorescence area due to over-irrigation in the districts of western Uttar Pradesh. The use of gypsum arrived later towards the end of the 19th century. In the Post-Independence period, sodic reclamation started in 1949 in the districts of central and western regions of the state. It is estimated that about 1.57 lakh hectares of saline land had been reclaimed by the end of 1993-94 in the state (Government of Uttar Pradesh, 2002).

In 1993-94, Uttar Pradesh Land Development Corporation (UPLDC) took up the challenge for reclaiming sodic lands with the initiation of World Bank funded project entitled, "UP Sodic Lands Reclamation Projects". During 1993-2001, of phase I, UPLDC reclaimed 68.4 thousands hectares of sodic land in 12 districts of the State with an investment of ₹ 313.71 crores during 1993-1999. Most of the expenditure was borne by the project authority, whereas farmers contributed in terms of their own labour in the reclamation activity. The community-reclaimed lands were distributed to the landless farmers. Hence, reclamation of saline land has enhanced employment as well as income of landless farmers and women (Government of Uttar Pradesh, 2001). In Phase II of UPSLRP funded by World Bank, 17 districts were selected for reclaiming nearly 2.18 lakh hectares with a budget of ₹ 1,469 crores. However, nearly 1.95 lakh hectares was reclaimed by covering nearly 3,611 villages up to December 2005. The main objective of the project was to reduce poverty in the rural areas through sustainable reclamation of sodic land using participatory approach (Government of Uttar Pradesh, 2006). Similarly, manifold benefits in terms of employment generation, increase of annual household income, reduction of labour migration occurred in the sodic land reclamation districts.

With the initiation of various programmes such as Drought Prone Area Programme (DPAP), Integrated Wasteland Development Programme (IWDP), National Watershed Development Project for Rainfed Areas (NWDPRA), Watershed Development Fund (WDF) by NABARD in the country, the State has greatly benefited by the combination of all these programmes. During the Ninth Plan, nearly 630 micro watersheds were developed covering 2.14 lakh hectares of land in different parts of rainfed areas of the State (Nayak, 2006). However, nearly 1.80 lakh hectares of land was developed for cultivation with the help of DPAP and NWDPRA in the State during the Ninth Plan. Similarly, substantial efforts were made to practice dry farming through improved drought assistance seeds and afforestation in the state.

Keeping in view the above background, the major objective of the study is to focus on the changing scenario of the cropping pattern, production, productivity and net gain under reclaimed condition to that of non-reclaimed conditions. Further, employment generation in the reclaimed and non-reclaimed villages is also covered under this study.

Coverage of the Study Area, Sample Size and Data: We have selected three districts covering one district from each region based on two conditions. Firstly, existence of sodicity and reclamation works being done subsequently. Secondly, some of the affected villages might be due to canal irrigation in at least one district and reclamation work being done subsequently. The purpose of selecting such areas is to test the hypothesis of higher productivity in areas of conjunctive use of canal irrigation as well as tube well irrigation in reclaimed villages. The comparison can be made for testing the productivity of areas, where conjunctive use of irrigation is not adopted. But both the situations might be coming under sodicity reclaimed villages. Keeping in mind these problems, we selected Sultanpur from eastern region, Raebareli from Central region and Mainpuri from Western region of the state. However, it is considered that Sultanpur and Raebareli districts are under the command areas of Sarada Sahayak canal, where sodicity is a problem due to water logging and subsequent reclamation works have been carried out. On the other hand, sodicity villages would be taken from Mainpuri district in Western region, where sodicity in not due to water logging and subsequent reclamation works are also done.

The selection of sample villages is based on the availability of sodic land affected villages and reclaimed villages. However, we have selected two blocks in each district constituting six blocks in all the three districts. The study focused on two sets of land, viz., reclaimed land and sodic affected land. In the category of reclaimed villages, we have selected two villages from each block consisting of a total of 12 villages in all the six blocks. The total sample size is restricted to 480 from all the 12 villages of six blocks in three districts.

Analysis of Economic Sustainability of Sodic Affected Areas

Cropping Pattern, Intensity, Productivity and Net Profit: The prevalent cropping pattern is the cumulative result of the past and present decisions by individuals, communities or government and their agencies in any locality. The decisions are usually based on experience, tradition, expected profit, personal preference and availability of resources, social and political pressures (ICAR, 2006). However, cropping pattern and intensity plays a crucial role in enhancement of profit, employment and eventually, reduction in poverty in a particular region. Cropping pattern is the proportion of area under various crops at a point of time. Cropping pattern is a dynamic concept as it changes over space and time. It is closely influenced by the geo-climatic, socio-cultural, economic, historical and political factors in a region (Husain, 1996).

Here, the extent of changes in cropping pattern in a reclaimed area is mainly due to irrigation facility over time. It also differentiates the extent of the changes in cropping pattern with and without reclamation. Cropping intensity means the variations in the density of any crop in an area or region at a given point of time. The concentration of a crop in an area largely depends on its terrain, temperature, moisture and pedagogical conditions. It studies percentage share of a crop in the total cropped area and the determination of relative density with the help of location quotient—some of the technical tools that are frequently used for the demarcation of command area.

Change in cropping pattern has been measured for some of the important crops out of total cultivated land among the surveyed samples in both reclaimed and affected land. It is observed that paddy and wheat are the two dominant crops in both the situation. However, paddy is the single most dominant crop constituting nearly 92 percent and 76 percent of the total cultivated area in reclaimed as well as non-reclaimed land respectively (Table 4.1). Similarly, wheat is the second important crop constituting nearly 90 percent and 59 percent in reclaimed and non-reclaimed land respectively. However, mustard is the third largest crop in reclaimed land, whereas it is bajra in the non-reclaimed land. Moreover, mustard and masoor are also another two important crops in the non-reclaimed areas. Therefore, cropping pattern clearly reveals that the farming class is mostly cultivating paddy and wheat, whereas other category of crops are cultivated for own requirement. One important factor is that the area under cultivation has shifted towards paddy and wheat after reclamation in the study area.

Table 4.1: Area under Cultivation of Different Crops in Reclaimed and Non-Reclaimed Villages (in percent)

	Reclaimed Land				Non-Reclaimed Land			
Crops	Rae Bareli	Sultan-pur	Main-puri	Average	Rae Bareli	Sultan-pur	Main-puri	Average
Paddy	92.1	94.41	88.9	91.7	85.7	70.7	70.5	75.5
Maize	1.5	0.0	0.4	0.6	0.5	0.7	0.0	0.4
Jowar	0.0	0.0	0.8	0.3	0.9	0.0	0.0	0.3
Wheat	87.7	90.7	90.3	89.8	49.9	46.1	79.4	58.6
Bajra	0.0	0.0	1.2	0.4	0.0	0.0	20.7	6.9
Arhar	0.5	0.2	0.0	0.2	0.5	2.1	0.0	0.9
Masoor	0.3	0.0	0.0	0.1	1.1	7.1	0.0	2.8
Urd	4.2	0.0	0.2	1.2	1.1	0.0	0.0	0.3
Mustard	0.8	10.3	1.8	4.6	0.8	10.6	0.1	3.9
Sugarcane	0.5	1.3	0.0	0.6	0.2	0.0	0.0	0.1
Potato	0.7	0.1	0.1	0.3	0.1	0.2	0.0	0.1
Onion	0.0	0.5	0.0	0.2	0.4	0.0	0.0	0.1
Garlic	0.0	0.0	1.1	0.4	0.0	0.0	2.1	0.7

Source: Estimated from Field Survey Data.

Cropping intensity shows that there has been a substantial shift of intensity of crops from non-reclaimed land to reclaimed land.

However, cropping intensity in the reclaimed land is 191 percent, whereas it is the highest in Sultanpur followed by Rae Bareli and Mainpuri (Table 4.2). This is one of the important improvements of reclamation of sodic land in the fragile region of the state. The cropping intensity of non-reclaimed land still looks higher at 151.67, because of irrigation facility in those villages.

Table 4.2: District-wise Cropping Intensity in Reclaimed and Non-Reclaimed Villages

	Rae Bareli	Sultanpur	Mainpuri	Total
Reclaimed Land				
GCA	329.14	464.46	476.97	1270.57
NCA	173.52	233.94	255.04	662.5
CI	189.69	198.54	187.02	191.79
Non-Reclaimed Land				
GCA	130.9	135.41	168.6	434.91
NCA	92.22	98.22	96.3	286.74
CI	141.95	137.89	175.08	151.67

Source: Estimated from Field Survey Data.

Productivity: The productivity of various important crops clearly reveals that here has been a substantial improvement of per acre production in reclaimed land over the non-reclaimed land in the villages of our study. However, the productivity of the reclaimed land for various major crops has been still lower than the productivity of normal land (Table 4.3). Paddy and wheat are the two important crops, which have shown substantial improvement over the non-reclaimed land but still lower than that of normal land. Sugarcane is the only crop, which has shown better performance in reclaimed land over the normal land. Moreover, per acre productivity of paddy and wheat in reclaimed land under this study is substantially lower than that of paddy and wheat in the reclaimed land of our earlier study (Nayak et al., 2007). [1] It is due the fact that the process of selection of villages in the earlier study was different from the process of selection of this study. The selection of villages in the earlier study was mostly biased towards the best villages in each district as the criteria adopted by the project authority. Therefore, it may be attributed here that productivity in the reclaimed land never equaled to normal land as it was shown otherwise in the earlier study. Moreover, the productivity of paddy and wheat is not at the highest level everywhere, as this study differs from our earlier observation.

Table 4.3: Productivity of Various Crops under Various Types of Soils (per acre)

Crops	Normal	Reclaimed	Affected
Paddy	13.67	9.01	5.31
Maize	8.58	4.11	2.61
Jowar	5.00	3.00	1.81
Wheat	9.15	5.87	3.83
Bajra	10.85	7.33	2.00
Arhar	1.74	1.84	0.28
Masoor	1.46	1.52	0.35
Urd	1.21	1.23	1.00
Mustard	1.60	0.40	0.44
Sugarcane	95.33	98.81	6.25
Potato	58.68	18.99	2.71
Onion	13.26	5.50	1.47
Peas	3.05	2.48	1.76
Garlic	23.73	17.86	13.50

Source: Estimated from Field Survey Data.

Total value of crops influence the changes in cropping pattern. However, paddy and wheat are the two important crops, not influenced much by the price of other high valued crops. It is apparent here that nearly 90 percent of the total cropped areas were under paddy and wheat in respective seasons as shown earlier. The values of respective crops are estimated with the help of current year prices collected from the field. It is clear that though the total value of garlic, potato, sugarcane is higher compared to the total value of paddy, wheat and other crops, still the area under cultivation of these crops is relatively lower. It is portrayed here that the total value of various crops in normal land is highest followed by reclaimed land and affected land as it has a direct linkage with productivity (Table 4.4). However, sugarcane, garlic and potato look more lucrative crops in both reclaimed and normal land. A very meager amount of total values is attached with the crops in affected land.

Table 4.4: Crop-wise Per Acre Value of Productivity under various types of Land (in ₹)

Crops	Normal	Reclaimed	Affected
Paddy	8629.36	5712.94	3340.56
Maize	5612.95	3405.48	2478.26
Jowar	3750.00	3150.00	2006.02
Wheat	8365.45	5347.82	3558.39
Bajra	7511.32	4800.00	1460
Arhar	4124.92	6250.00	761.68
Masoor	3224.35	1590.91	722.5
Urd	2740.66	2346.94	1800
Mustard	3455.77	810.33	906.61
Sugarcane	11905.67	16250.00	3750
Potato	22675.20	9329.61	735.29
Onion	7436.71	5083.33	1176.47
Peas	4580.45	3267.33	2647.6
Garlic	24895.52	18142.86	13500

Source: Estimated from Field Survey Data.

Net Income/Profit of the Reclaimed Land: Net income of some of the important crops is estimated both in reclaimed and non-reclaimed land. [2] However, net profits of these crops are estimated by taking into consideration the total value and total operation costs of the respective crop. Total values of various crops is estimated by taking into consideration the per acre productivity and market prices of various crops, which were collected from the field. Total cost of various crops was estimated by taking five major components of costs, namely: (a) seeds, (b) fertilizers, (c) wages and employment, (d) machine labour, and (e) irrigation charges etc. However, fertilizers are decomposed into major two parts, viz.: (a) organic manures, and (b) chemical fertilizers and pesticides. Similarly, wages and employment part is the combination of family labour and hired labour.

The extent of net profit for major crops was estimated in the reclaimed as well as non-reclaimed land. However, the paddy and wheat being the two dominant crops, their net profit per acre was ₹ 2,909 and ₹ 2,464 respectively in the reclaimed land (Table 4.5). These are the only two crops, where net profits are moderate and spread over all the districts. However, some of the crops, viz. garlic, potato, maize are more profitable crops in the reclaimed land but by only few acres of land in a district. In case of other crops, estimation of net profit is not clear. For example, mustard is mostly cultivated along with wheat in the rabi season. The cost of production of mustard is attached to the cost of wheat because wheat is a major crop. The level of net income is very much higher for most of the crops in reclaimed land than that of in the non-reclaimed land (Table 4.5). It is mainly due to low productivity with low valued crops in the affected land. Moreover, the level of investment in the crops of affected land was also lower compared to that of in the reclaimed land.

So far as the land holding size and net income for paddy is concerned, it is observed that marginal farmers are the highest beneficiaries followed by small, semi-medium, medium and large farmers. But the per acre productivity of the same crop is highest for medium farmers followed by semi-medium, marginal, small and large farmers. Therefore, it may be attributed here, that marginal small farmers get more benefits not due to higher productivity but due to low investment/high self induced investment compared to medium and large farmers.

Table 4.5: District-wise Net Income in Reclaimed Land (in ₹)

Crops	Rae Bareli	Sultan-pur	Main-puri	Average	Rae Bareli	Sultan-pur	Main-puri	Average
	Reclaimed Land				Non-Reclaimed Land			
Paddy	2509	2660	3434	2909	898	1588	2422	1541
Bajra	-2362	1114	1149	1953	-1794	NA	363	270
Wheat	2212	2161	3137	2464	645	1938	1968	1898
Mustard	1262	2133	1149	1979	268	723	NA	547
Barley	2660	NA	3363	3184	NA	NA	1358	1559
Potato	3447	14736	2900	7149	8593	3492	NA	5356
Urd	1597	NA	NA	2089	NA	NA	NA	NA
Garlic	724	833	11143	15713	NA	525	7363	2420
Arhar	9986	-2071	NA	3669	NA	694	NA	700
Maize	NA	NA	3855	3160	NA	NA	NA	NA

Source: Estimated from Field Survey Data.

The per acre contribution of family labour is higher in case of marginal and small farmers (Table 4.6). Net income or profit for wheat is highest for medium farmers followed by small, semi-medium, marginal and large farmers as it is consistent with the productivity of farmers based on land holding size. Though, garlic and potato are some of the profitable crops, yet the production is very much little for the land covered by each farmer.

It is observed that the net income per acre of various crops in non-reclaimed land is definitely lower than the reclaimed land. However, the marginal farmers earned the highest in paddy followed by small, semi-medium and medium farmers. In case of wheat, medium farmers had the highest net profit followed by small, marginal and semi-medium farmers (Table

4.7). The net profit in non-reclaimed land was consistent with the reclaimed land, though the magnitude is different.

Table 4.6: Land Holding Size-wise Net Income in Reclaimed Land (in ₹)

Crops	Marginal	Small	Semi-Medium	Medium	Large	Total
Paddy	3208	3076	3036	2132	157	2910
Bajra	2394	2292	-3120	NA	NA	1953
Wheat	2221	2503	2049	3106	NA	2464
Mustard	1556	1960	1582	3970	3634	-1979
Barley	5995	2854	2289	NA	NA	3740
Potato	9880	3614	14736	-3117	NA	7149
Urd	55	2237	NA	NA	NA	2089
Garlic	22097	9866	-952	NA	NA	15713
Arhar	6919	10946	-2071	NA	NA	3669
Maize	4512	1837	NA	NA	NA	3160

Source: Estimated from Field Survey Data.

Table 4.7: Land holding size wise Net Profit in Non-Reclaimed Land (in ₹)

Crops	Marginal	Small	Semi-medium	Medium	Total
Paddy	2128	1553	1254	616	1541
Bajra	160	NA	1419	NA	270
Wheat	1857	1919	1434	2878	1898
Mustard	802	-1512	NA	NA	507
Barley	1459	NA	NA	NA	1662
Garlic	11183	8477	132	413	2420

Source: Estimated from Field Survey Data.

Extent and Dimension of Employment in Reclaimed and Non-reclaimed Land

The promotion of employment after reclaiming the sodic affected land is one of the major important objectives of the project authority for the overall development of the fragile regions. One way of promoting the employment is that when salt affected lands are distributed among the landless and marginal farmers, the reclamation process begins. In general, the extent of investment and employment is higher with the expectation of higher productivity than that of non-reclaimed land (Joshi, 1996). Under such circumstances, employment and equity issues override pure efficiency considerations that apply to good soils. The employment pattern of the reclaimed and non-reclaimed soils under our study can be assessed through two stages of analysis. Firstly, it can be assessed by analyzing the man-days of employment at the family level both in reclaimed and non-reclaimed households. Secondly, the employment pattern can be judged in terms of investment for agricultural production of various crops, such as family labour, hired labour and bullock and machine labour. Moreover, this aspect can be substantiated by estimating the magnitude of total investment per unit of land and its respective share in both types of lands.

So far as labour employment for the production of various crops in both reclaimed and non-reclaimed land is concerned, there are two types of labour employed, i.e., employment of family labour and labour on hired basis. Family labour is a major source of employment in agricultural land as most of marginal, small, semi-medium and medium farmers contribute their own labour in their respective land. Large farmers normally employ labour on hire basis irrespective of the time required for crop growth. However, medium and semi-medium farmers employ labour on hired basis in their agricultural land in the busy season to cater the need of finishing the required work in time. This study clearly reveals that family labour has a larger share for any kind of crops in both reclaimed as well as non-reclaimed land. For example, there is a need for 40 labourers per acre for paddy in the reclaimed land, whereas it is only 6 labourers on hired basis.

Similar trend (the number of family labour in reclaimed land is higher than that of non-reclaimed land) is observed for all other crops in both types of land (Table 4.8). Most importantly, per acre family labour required for paddy cultivation is almost the same both in reclaimed and non-reclaimed land. Secondly, per acre labour requirement for other crops in non-reclaimed land is lower than that of reclaimed land. Similar types of results are observed in reclaimed and non-reclaimed land for hired labour category, i.e., per acre hired labour is lower in most of the crops. In other words, farmers dared to afford more family as well as hired labour in reclaimed land than in the non-reclaimed land, simply because of higher expectations of output.

Table 4.8: Crop-wise and Type-wise Labour Employment (Man-days)

Crops	Family Labour			Hired Labour		
	Re-claimed	Non-reclaimed	Average	Re-claimed	Non-reclaimed	Average
Paddy	40.32	40.57	40.38	5.81	3.15	5.19
Bajra	29.72	18.18	26.21	1.27	0.71	1.10
Wheat	26.14	20.53	25.04	1.68	0.89	1.52
Mustard	19.85	18.99	19.67	4.66	1.35	4.02
Barley	20.94	13.33	15.42	0.94	0.00	0.75
Potato	34.99	29.11	33.03	0.00	0.00	0.00
Urd	30.22	15.00	14.17	0.00	0.00	0.00
Garlic	35.63	17.53	27.87	2.65	0.00	2.35
Arhar	26.95	5.00	24.21	5.27	0.00	4.61
Maize	25.75	8.1	16.92	0.00	0.00	0.00

Source: Estimated from Field Survey Data.

Land holding-wise labour employment in the form of family labour and hired labour clearly reveals that paddy is the dominant crop, which requires maximum labourers followed by potato, wheat, garlic etc. Secondly, per acre family labour for any type of crop is highest for marginal farmers followed by small, semi-medium, medium and large farmers (Table 4.9). Thirdly, the reverse tendency is followed in case of hired labour, i.e., highest number of hired labour is required per acre by large farmers followed by medium, semi-medium and so on.

Table 4.9: Crop-wise and Land Holding Size-wise Labour Employment (Man-days)

Crops	Marginal	Small	Semi-medium	Medium	Large	Average
Family Labour						
Paddy	51.15	37.44	18.39	8.47	1.43	40.38
Bajra	27.48	34.32	15.5	0	NA	26.21
Wheat	28.06	26.98	14.64	5.39	NA	25.04
Mustard	24.15	16.52	17	6.16	2.14	19.67
Barley	23.9	30.92	11	11	NA	15.42
Potato	65	40.83	14.92	0	NA	33.03
Urd	19.05	33.94	50	0	NA	14.17
Garlic	31.2	41.37	4.67	13.33	NA	27.87
Arhar	28.89	10.61	29.83	5	NA	24.21
Maize	71.17	42.68	NA	NA	NA	16.92
Hired Labour						
Paddy	1.82	6.2	11.63	15.95	18.88	5.19
Bajra	0.26	1.6	1	0	10.64	1.1
Wheat	0.59	1.28	5.5	2.63		1.52
Mustard	0.34	2.18	13.68	9.49	0.29	4.02
Barley	0.61	0	4.5	0	NA	0.75
Potato	0	0	0	0	NA	0
Urd	0	0	0	0	NA	0
Garlic	3.33	1.96	0	0	NA	2.35
Arhar	0	0	7.37	0	NA	4.61
Maize	0	0	0	0	NA	0

Source: Estimated from Field Survey Data.

Summary and Conclusions

So far as cropping pattern in concerned, paddy is the single most dominant crop, which constitutes nearly 92 percent and 76 percent of the total cultivated area in reclaimed and non-reclaimed land respectively. Wheat is the second important crop constituting nearly 90 percent and 59 percent in reclaimed and non-reclaimed land respectively. The cropping intensity reveals that there has been a substantial increase of intensity of crops from non-reclaimed land to reclaimed land. The productivity of various important crops clearly reveals that there has been a substantial improvement of per acre production in reclaimed land over the non-reclaimed land in the villages under study. However, the productivity of the reclaimed land for various major crops has been still lower than the productivity of normal land.

Further, the study reveals that family labour has larger share for any kind of crops in both reclaimed as well as non-reclaimed land. The per acre family labour for all other crops except paddy has increased in reclaimed land over non-reclaimed land. Moreover, per acre hired labour is lower than that of family labour in both reclaimed and non-reclaimed land.

End Notes

1. The productivity of paddy and wheat is 12 quintals and 9 quintals respectively in the reclaimed land of our earlier study.
2. Net income or profit per unit of land has been estimated by deducting the total costs per acre out of total value in the year based on the information from the field. The methodology for measurement of costs has been followed the methods adopted by Costs and Price Commission, Ministry of Agriculture, Government of India.

References

Abrol, I.P. (1984), Alkali Soils and Their Management: A Case Study from India, Twelfth International Congress on Irrigation and Drainage, Vol. 1 (B), Fort Collins, US.

Datta, K.K. and Bhu Dayal (2000), Irrigation with Poor Quality Water: An Empirical Study of Input Use, Economic Loss and Coping Strategy, *Indian Journal of Agricultural Economics*, Vol. 55, No. 1, January-March.

Dinakar, V.S.. (1993), Salinity and Reclamation in Water Management, in Seminar on Irrigation Water Management, Water Management Forum, New Delhi.

Government of Uttar Pradesh (2001), Uttar Pradesh Sodic Land Reclamation Project, Vol. I, Uttar Pradesh Bhumi Sudhar Nigam, Lucknow.

Government of Uttar Pradesh, (2002), *Report on Sarda Sahayak Command Area*, Ministry of Irrigation, Command Area Development Office, Government of Uttar Pradesh, Lucknow.

Government of Uttar Pradesh, (2006), *Uttar Pradesh Sodic Land Reclamation-II*, Uttar Pradesh Bhumi Sudhar Nigam, Status Report, Lucknow.

Husain, M. (1996), *Agricultural Geography*, Rawat Publications, New Delhi.

ICAR, (2006), *Handbook of Agriculture*, New Delhi.

Joshi, P.K. (1987), Effects of Surface Irrigation on Land Degradation: Problems and Strategies, *Indian Journal of Agricultural Economics,* Vol. 42, No. 3, July-September.

Joshi, P.K. (1996), Farmer Investments and Government Intervention in Salt affected and Waterlogged Soils, in Kerr, John; Dinesh K. Marothia; Katar Singh; C. Ramasamy and William R. Bentley (eds.), *Natural Resource Economics: Theory and Application in India*, Oxford and IBH Publishing Co. Pvt. Ltd, New Delhi.

Joshi, P.K. and A.K. Agnihotri (1984), An Assessment of the Adverse Effects of Canal Irrigation in India, *Indian Journal of Agricultural Economics*, Vol. XXXIX, No. 3, July-September.

Joshi, P.K. and Dayananda Jha (1992), An Economic Inquiry into the Impact of Soil Alkalinity and Waterlogging, *Indian Journal of Agricultural Economics*, Vol. 47, No. 2, April-June.

Nayak, Sanatan, (2002), Extent and Costs of Environmental Degradation in Sriramsagar Project Command Area: Integration with Cost Benefit Analysis, *Artha Vijnan*, Vol. XLIV, Nos. 3-4, September-December.

Nayak, (2006), *Waterlogging in Eastern Region of Uttar Pradesh: Extent, Causes and Policy Interventions,* Paper presented in the National Seminar on "Conservation, Management and Development of Land Resources with Special Reference to Eastern Region of Uttar Pradesh", at G.B. Pant Social Science Institute, Allahabad, 9th-10th March, 2006.

Nayak, Sanatan (2006), Environmental Degradation to Land Resources, *Review of Development and Change,* Vol. XI, No. 1.

Nayak, Sanatan, G.S. Mehta, A.K. Singh, (2007), *Study on The Impact and Effectiveness of Training and Capacity Building*

Undertaken under the U.P. Sodic Land Reclamation Project-II, submitted to UPBSN, Giri Institute of Development Studies, Lucknow.

Report of Soil Testing (2008), Government of Uttar Pradesh, Soil Testing Centre, Department of Agriculture, Alambagh, Lucknow.

5

An Economic Analysis of Cutting Edge Technology in Rice Cultivation

Surajit Haldar, Honnaiah, Sowmyashree B.V. and Abhiram Dash

Introduction

It was an innovation in the yields, i.e. the Green Revolution during mid-1960s that catalyzed a metamorphosis from the conditions of food shortage to one of self-sufficiency and beyond, making India in the process, a world leader in the production of agricultural commodities. Rice production at global level has increased from 605 million tonnes in 2004 to 696 million tonnes in 2010, where 90 percent of the same is produced and consumed in Asia only (FASTAT, 2010). Among all the countries, India is the second biggest rice producing country after China which produced 89.13 million tonnes in 2010-11. In India, rice is an important ingredient of a household food basket, yet its yield level is low, stagnant and uncertain (Barah, 2009). The enhancement in rice production has been mainly due to high yielding varieties, while harvested rice area for the corresponding period has expanded from 31 million ha. to about 44 million ha., accounting for only 42 percent increase. However, to maintain the present level of self-sufficiency, India needs to produce 115 million tonnes of rice by the year 2020 which can be brought either by horizontal or vertical expansion (Department of Agriculture, Government of India, 2011).

In India, the Green Revolution was oriented towards high input usage, particularly fertilizers, irrigation and plant protection chemicals. As a result of excessive inputs use especially ground water, the cost of cultivation has escalated. Besides inefficiency in resource use, the yield also stagnated in many parts of rice growing regions in India. There is little scope to increase the area, hence increase in production and productivity with an improvement in efficiency of production through technological breakthrough to meet the growing demand is required. As changing climatic conditions are becoming more unfavourable for rice cultivation, there is a strong need of water saving rice cultivation technology that not only reduces the cost of cultivation but also contributes less in green house gas (GHG) emission that causes a major adverse effect on ozone layer.

Interestingly, some improved management practices like system of rice intensification (SRI) was implemented in many parts of India. The SRI is a system of production of rice, considered to be a disembodied technological breakthrough in paddy cultivation. It involves the application of certain management practices, which together provide better growing condition for rice plants, particularly in the root zone, than for those plants grown under conventional practices. In fact, SRI is a less water consuming method of rice cultivation when compared to rice cultivation in farmers' method, semi-dry method and rotational method of rice cultivation in Krishna western delta command area of Andhra Pradesh (Radha et al., 2009). Thus, SRI can be a more suitable method of rice cultivation for poor farmers who have relatively more labour than land and capital.

The system of rice intensification (SRI) has been practiced since decades mainly for higher yield and qualitative grain and fodder production. Besides, SRI method confers a degree of protection against climatic hazards and also against losses from pests and diseases. Such effects could derive from the larger, deeper, longer-lived root systems that SRI practices elicit, and from the greater fertility and water-holding capacity of soil systems managed, according to SRI recommendations. In SRI method, rice plants can produce more than twice as much photosynthate per unit of water transpired (Uphoff et al., 2009). Such water efficiency will become more important in the decades ahead.

Problem Statement

Being an important rice growing state in India, West Bengal has grown 147.20 lakh tonnes of rice in 57.20 lakh hectares of land during 2007-08. Bardhaman district known as rice bowl of West Bengal cultivated an area of 6.35 lakh hectares (11 percent of state rice area) of rice with the production at 27.8 lakh tonnes (19 percent of total state production) in 2007-08, achieving a record productivity level of 4385 kg./ha.; almost twice the state average productivity level (2593 kg./ha.). Of late, the shortage of water has become a hindering factor for rice cultivation.

Hence, concerted efforts were made to introduce water saving technique like system of rice intensification (SRI) method of rice cultivation in major rice growing districts of West Bengal. Presently, SRI method is being practiced in 15 districts of West Bengal, mainly to combat water shortage especially during *rabi* and summer season. Keeping in view the above issues, an attempt was made to study the comparative economics of SRI method of rice cultivation vis-à-vis conventional method during *rabi* season. In *rabi* season, rice cultivation is mainly dependent on ground water, where exorbitant extraction of it has led to not only scarcity of drinking water in summer season but also conventional method has been emitting enormous amount of GHGs hampering climate to a large extent. In this regard, an economic analysis of SRI method of rice cultivation was assessed as against conventional method of rice cultivation in nursery and main field separately. Further, technical and allocative efficiency level of farmers was also assessed using Timmer's measure of technical efficiency. Logit analysis was also employed for analysing the factors that influence the choice among alternatives. In the present study, to know the factors influencing adoption of SRI method of rice cultivation, binary logistic regression was used.

It was hypothesized that: (a) SRI method of rice cultivation is more profitable than conventional method, and (b) return per rupee of expenditure is significantly higher in SRI method compared to the conventional method.

Methodology

In West Bengal state, the highest rice producing Bardhaman district was selected purposively. Random sampling technique was adopted for selecting blocks, villages and farmers. In Bardhaman district, four blocks (Ausgram-I, Ausgram-II, Bhatar, Galsi-I) were selected randomly. In each block, 15 farmers were randomly selected constituting 60 farmers each under SRI and conventional method of rice cultivation. Thus, 120 sample farmers were interviewed personally with structured schedules. The farm management cost concept was used for evaluating crop profitability. Production function analysis was employed to analyse efficiency of rice production. Timmer's measure of technical efficiency was employed to measure the efficiency of rice cultivation in different method of rice cultivation. Logit analysis was employed for analysing the factors that influence the choice among alternatives. In the present study, to know the factors influencing adoption of SRI method of rice cultivation, binary logistic regression was used. The variables and their expected signs are summarized in Table 5.1.

The dependent variable is 1, if the farmer has adopted SRI method, otherwise it is 0. Expected sign explains hypothesis made on the variables. Age of the respondent is hypothesized to have negative influence on adoption of SRI method. Farmers from higher age group may be more conservative and they may not switch their farming system from conventional to SRI. Education is supposed to have positive influence, because with the increase in educational qualifications, the awareness about SRI increases. With the increase in per capita income, the farmer has option to go for mechanization of his farm and hence he can adopt improved techniques like SRI method of rice cultivation. If a farmer has membership in any co-operative, which facilitates credit or any other means of financial support, it is hypothesized that it will have a positive influence on the adoption of SRI method. With the increase in the distance from the canals, farmers tend to manage water more judiciously and thus it is hypothesized that the probability of adoption of SRI method is more.

Table 5.1: Variables Used in the Logit Analysis and their Expected Signs

Independent Variables	Description of the Variables	Expected Sign
Age	Age of the respondent (in years)	-
Education	No. of years of schooling	+
Per capita income	Per capita income of the respondent (in ₹)	+
Membership	1, if the respondent has membership in a co-operative, 0 otherwise	+
Contacts	1, if the respondent has frequent contact with extension agents, 0 otherwise	+
Distance	Distance of the farm from the canal (in km.)	+

Results and Discussion

As there are differences in nursery management between conventional and SRI methods in *rabi* season, the resource use pattern and expenditure made were analyzed separately and then the total cost return analysis was employed.

Nursery Management: The input use pattern and cost incurred on different inputs in nursery management of both the methods is presented in Table 5.2. In SRI method, nursery area (117.3 m^2) was about one fourth as compared to the conventional method (565.6 m^2) in *rabi* season. The expenditure on labour input service was comparatively higher in conventional method (₹ 2,066) as compared to the SRI method (₹ 582)—this saved a total of ₹ 2,135 as expenditure of SRI for nursery bed preparation over the conventional one.

Short duration nursery (8 to 12 days), meagre quantity of water application (just to keep optimum moisture level) and other inputs used in SRI nursery were the major advantages over conventional methods (25 days of nursery), that reduced the total nursery cost by ₹ 3,508 as against the conventional method.

Table 5.2: Input Use Pattern and Cost of Raising Nursery for Rice Cultivation in *Rabi* Season

Particulars	Conventional		SRI	
	Qty.	Value (₹)	Qty.	Value (₹)
Area (sq. meter)	563.6		117.3	
Seed (kg.)	41.7	692	8.4	142(550)
FYM (tonnes)	0.3	94	0.1	24(70)
Rice husk ash (tonnes)			0.3	78(78*)
N (kg.)	16.6	210	4.7	40(170)
P (kg.)	4.3	108	0.0	0(108)
K (kg.)	16.0	212	4.1	54(158)
PPC (ml.)	208.2	281	15.3	35(246)
Man-days	17.2	1545	4.1	338(1207)
Bullock pair	2.0	507	0.6	158(347)
Machine hours	1.8	665	0.2	86(579)
Total labour cost		2717		582(2135)
Electricity and fuel charges		290		40(250)
Total cost		4503		995(3508)

Note: 1. Nursery area is for transplanting one hectare; 2. Figures in parentheses are savings in SRI method over conventional method in Rupees (₹); 3. *Indicates excess in SRI method over conventional method; and 4. Qty. denotes quantity.

Costs and Returns Structure in Conventional and SRI Method of Rice Cultivation in *Rabi* Season: The per hectare cost in SRI cultivation was lower (₹ 43,862) compared to conventional method (₹ 44,853) and the similar findings were also recorded by Uprety in Nepal (2004) and Vishnudas in Kerala (2006).

Table 5.3: Input Use Pattern in Conventional and SRI Method of Rice Cultivation in *Rabi* Season (per ha.)

(value in ₹)

Particulars	Conventional		SRI		Percent change
	Quantity	Value	Quantity	Value	
Variable cost					
Seeds	41.7	692 (1.5)	8.4	142 (0.3)	79.5
Fertilizer					
N	115.0	1426 (3.2)	105.1	1315 (3.0)	7.8
P	53.4	1685 (3.8)	48.1	1399 (3.2)	17.0
K	60.5	795 (1.8)	55.6	731 (1.7)	8.1
Farmyard manure	4.2	1463 (3.3)	8.3	2891 (6.6)	-97.6
Plant protection chemical	1758.7	3264 (7.3)	741.3	1480(3.4)	54.7
Human labour	183.5	14929 (33.3)	169.6	14778 (33.7)	1.0
Bullock labour	18.0	4590 (10.2)	16.3	4164 (9.5)	9.3
Machine labour	4.8	1895 (4.2)	3.6	1412 (3.2)	25.5
Electricity and fuel charges		1361 (3.0)		487 (1.1)	64.2
Total working capital		32101 (71.6)		28800 (65.7)	10.3
Interest on working capital @ 6 %		1926 (4.3)		1728 (3.9)	10.3
Total variable cost		34027 (75.9)		30528 (69.6)	10.3
Fixed cost					
Land revenue		18 (0.04)		18 (0.04)	0.0
Rental value of land		9438 (21.04)		12045 (27.5)	-27.6
Depreciation on machinery		1098 (2.5)		914 (2.1)	16.8
Interest on fixed capital @ 11 %		270 (0.6)		356 (0.8)	-32.0
total fixed cost		10825 (24.1)		13334 (30.4)	-23.2
Total cost of cultivation		44853		43862	-2.2
Main product (tonnes)	6.4	59208	8.3	80320	35.7
By-product (tonnes)	4.5	2141	6.3	3995	86.6
Total return		61349		84315	37.4
Net return		16496		40453	145.2
Total returns per rupee of total cost		1.37		1.92	

Note: 1. Figures in parentheses are percentage to the total cost. 2. Percent change indicates percentage change in expenditure to SRI method over conventional method.

High labour cost was major reason for higher per hectare cost of SRI paddy cultivation, whereas more expenditure on human labour (₹ 14,778) in SRI paddy was because of more labour required for careful transplantation of single seedlings and the frequent intercultural operation using rotary weeder.

The higher expenditure made on bullock and machine labour (₹ 4,164 and ₹ 1,412 respectively) was necessary in SRI method because of more number of levelling operations, line transplantation etc. Thus, it proves the hypothesis that labour input use is higher in SRI method as compared to conventional method (Table 5.3).

Expenditure made on plant protection chemical was comparatively less in SRI method as compared to conventional method while the expenditure incurred on irrigation in terms of electricity and fuel changes for SRI method (₹ 487) was very less than that in conventional method (₹ 1,361) in *rabi* season because of lesser requirement of irrigation and volume of water irrigated in SRI method. It was worth noting that even with high seed rate and more number of hills per meter square, the yield level (6.39 tonnes per ha.) was less in conventional method then that in SRI method (8.31 tonnes per ha.) in *rabi* season because of more number of effective tillers per meter square in SRI paddy. The per hectare cost of cultivation was also found to be lower in SRI compared to conventional method mainly because of higher paddy yield harvested in SRI method.

Thus, it proved the hypothesis that SRI method of rice cultivation is more profitable than conventional method. It could be further noticed that unit price of the paddy output and by-product realized by SRI farmer was also higher and this was due to superior quality of grain and fodder as compared to conventional method. It was also noted that considerable proportions of farmer even sell SRI produced output as seed that fetches higher per unit return. The gross returns per rupee of total cost in conventional method was ₹ 1.37 in conventional and ₹ 1.92 in SRI method, because of high gross returns in SRI method of rice cultivation (Table 5.3) and the similar findings were also recorded by Anjugam et al. (2008) in Tamil Nadu. Thus, it proves the hypothesis that return per rupee of expenditure is significantly higher in SRI method compared to the conventional method.

Technical and Allocative Efficiency in Conventional and SRI Methods of Rice Cultivation: The coefficients of multiple determinations (R^2) were 0.80 and 0.81 for estimated production function of conventional and SRI method in *rabi* season. The high and significant F values indicated that Cobb-Douglas production function was adequate in explaining 80 percent of the variation in output in conventional and SRI method due to variation in the resources included in the model. The constant returns to scale were noticed in both the methods since sum of elasticity coefficients were nearly one.

Scopes for intensification of resources were estimated by marginal value products (MVP) of resources and were compared with the respective marginal factor cost (MFC) (Table 5.4). The MVP-MFC ratio for labour (1.78) and plant nutrients (1.73) were more than 1 in both the methods, whereas the ratio for seed (0.40) was less than 1 in both the methods in *rabi* season. But MVP-MFC ratios for plant nutrients (1.73) and plant protection chemicals (1.57) were more than 1 in SRI than conventional methods. Hence, there is a scope for further increasing per hectare returns by increasing the usage of plant nutrients and plant protection chemicals.

Table 5.4: MVP and MFC Ratios of Resources in *Rabi* Season

Inputs	Conventional			SRI		
	MVP	MFC	Ratio	MVP	MFC	Ratio
Seed	0.94	1	0.94	1.61	1	1.61
Labour	1.46	1	1.46	1.07	1	1.07
Plant nutrients	1.33	1	1.33	1.73	1	1.73
Plant protection chemicals	1.35	1	1.35	1.57	1	1.57

The average technical efficiency for conventional and SRI farmers was 0.72 and 0.65 (Table 5.5). About 20 percent of conventional and 10 percent of SRI farmers were found to operate at technical efficiency rating between 0.71 and 0.75.

Whereas, about 10 percent of conventional farmers and 4 percent SRI farmers in *rabi* season were operating at technical efficiency rating above 0.90 respectively. The similar types of result were also recorded by Basavaraja et al. (2008) and Kumar et al. (2005).

In *rabi* season, the allocative efficiency and the economic efficiency was less in SRI method as compared to conventional method. In both the methods, farmers were operating at less allocative efficiency than the technical efficiency. Hence, it can be concluded that by overcoming the inefficiency (both technical and allocative) in conventional and SRI method of rice cultivation, the profits could be increased in the study area. Hence, more concerted efforts are needed to improve efficiency in both the methods of rice cultivation.

Table 5.5: Distribution of Farmers According to Technical Efficiency Rating Along with Allocative and Economic Efficiency

Percent Technical Efficiency Rating	Conventional	SRI
<= 70 percent	14 (46.67)	34 (68.00)
71-75 percent	6 (20.00)	5 (10.00)
76-80 percent	2 (6.67)	5 (10.00)
81-85 percent	3 (10.00)	1 (2.00)
86-90 percent	2 (6.67)	3 (6.00)
90 percent and above	3 (10.00)	2 (4.00)
Average technical efficiency	0.72	0.65
Allocative efficiency	0.68	0.56
Economic efficiency	0.49	0.36

Note: Figures in parentheses indicate percent to total.

Factor Influencing Adoption of SRI Method of Rice Cultivation: Binary logistic regression was run using SPSS

12.0 software and the results obtained are presented in Table 5.6.

Table 5.6: Results of Logit Analysis for Adopting SRI Method

Variable	Co-efficient	Significance	Exp(B)	P
Age	-0.532	0.175	1.702	0.630
Education	0.283***	0.009	39.723	0.430
Membership	10.724***	0.000	513.74	0.998
Per capita income	3.682*	0.071	0.753	0.975
Contacts	5.734**	0.024	0.03	0.029
Distance	2.393***	0.004	10.945	0.916
Constant	19.704**	0.017	0	
- 2 Log likelihood				26.83
Negelkerke R^2				81.5

Note: ***, ** and *denote significance at 1, 5 and 10 percent level of significance respectively.

Experience in farming in terms of age of the respondents was found to be negative but statistically insignificant. Farmers from higher age groups may be more conservative and they do not want to switch their farming system from conventional to SRI method. Education is influencing positively and the coefficient is highly significant. Thus, it implies that as the number of years of education increases, the farmers are keen to adopt new techniques like SRI than others. On the other hand, if years of education increased by one year than probability of adopting SRI increases by 0.43. The similar types of results were also recorded by Sitadevi and Ponnarsai (2009) in Tamil Nadu, Anjugam et al. (2008) and Barah (2009) in Tamil Nadu.

The distance of canal from the farm is also having a positive significant influence on the adoption of SRI. As the distance increases, the farmers are more efficient in using their input resources like water in production of rice. However, if the distance from canal increases by one kilometre than the probability of adopting SRI increases by 0.916. Therefore, for farmers who are far away from canals, the adoption level is higher than others. With the increase in per capita income, the farmers are more devoted for farm mechanization and are therefore adopting more SRI than others. Having membership in a co-operative or any other financial organization increases the probability of adoption of SRI method compared to others.

Conclusion

Besides the less resource use, the profitability (return per rupee) in SRI rice cultivation is higher vis-à-vis the conventional method. Hence, the farmers have to be educated and empowered through training and demonstrations. The efficiency level (both technical and allocative) in SRI is higher compared to conventional method in terms of water usage in nursery management as well as in main field. Logit regression analysis indicated that, educational level and the distance from the canal increases the probability of adopting the SRI method. Thus, SRI must be promoted from the climate resilient point of view. Hence, appropriate interventions like empowering farmers through training and demonstrations with proper guidance from extension personnel has to be made for larger adoption in the study area as well as throughout the water scarce areas.

References

Anjugam, M., Varadharaj, S. and Padmarani, S. (2008), Cost-Benefit Analysis of SRI Technique in Paddy Cultivation, Department of Agricultural Economics, Tamil Nadu, Coimbatore.

Barah, B.C. (2009), Economic and Ecological Benefits of System of Rice Intensification (SRI) in Tamil Nadu. *Agricultural Economics Research Review*, 22, pp. 209-214.

Basavaraja, H., Mahajanshetti, S.B. and Sivangaraju, P. (2008), Technological Change in Paddy Production: A Comparative Analysis of Traditional and SRI Method of Cultivation, *Indian Journal of Agricultural Economics*, 64, pp. 629-640.

Government of India, Department of Agriculture, 2011, New Delhi.

Kumar, L.R., Shrinivas, K. and Singh, S.R.K. (2005), Technical Efficiency in Rice Farms under Irrigated Conditions of

Northwest Himalayan Region-A Non-Parametric Approach. *Indian Journal of Agricultural Economics*, 60, pp. 483-493.

Radha, Y., Reddy, K.Y., Rao, G.S., Chandra and, S.R. and Babu, G.K. (2009), Water-saving Rice Production Technologies in Krishna Western Delta Command of Andhra Pradesh-An Economic Analysis, *Agricultural Economics Research Review*, 22, pp. 397-400.

Sitadevi, K. and Ponnarsi, T. (2009), An Economic Analysis of Modern Rice Production Technology and its Adoption Behaviour in Tamil Nadu, *Agricultural Economics Research Review*, 22, pp. 341-347.

Uphoff, N., Anas, I., Rupela, O.P., Thakur, A.K. and Thiyagarajan T.M. (2009), Learning about Positive Plant-microbial Interactions from the System of Rice Intensification (SRI), *Aspects of Applied Biology*, 98, pp. 29-54.

Uprety, R. (2005), Economic Analysis of System of Rice Intensification (SRI) Methods in Morang District of Nepal, Main Season, DADO Morang, Biratnagar, Nepal.

Vishnudas, C.K. (2006), SRI Trials in Wayanad-Experiences of RASTA, LEISA India, 8, pp. 16-17.

6

Understanding Organic Farming: Potential and Constraints

Jeeban Jyoti Mohanty

Introduction

Organic agriculture is a form of agriculture that relies on ecosystem management and attempts to reduce or eliminate external agricultural input, especially synthetic ones. It is a holistic production management system that promotes and enhances agro-ecosystem's health, including biodiversity, biological cycles and soil biological activity. Organic farming is not a new concept in India. Indian farmers have the distinction of using organic in agriculture from times immemorial. Several forms of organic farming are being successfully practiced in diverse climate, particularly in rain fed, tribal, mountains and hill areas of the country. Among all farming systems, organic farming is gaining wide attention among farmers, entrepreneurs, policy makers and agricultural scientists for varied reasons such as it minimizes the dependence on chemical inputs (fertilizers, pesticides, herbicides and other agro-chemicals) and thus safeguards/improves quality of resources and the environment. It is labour intensive and provides an opportunity to increase rural employment and achieve long-term improvements in the quality of resource base.

Codex Alimentarius Commission, a joint body of FAO/WHO defines "organic agriculture as holistic food production management systems, which promotes and enhances agro-ecosystem's health including biodiversity, biological cycles and soil biological activity". Organic production systems are based on specific standards precisely formulated for food production and aim at achieving agro-ecosystems which are socially and ecologically sustainable. Many definitions have been proposed for organic agriculture with primary focus on ecological principles as the basis for crop production and animal husbandry. It emphasizes more on optimising the yield potential of crops and livestock under a given set of farming conditions rather than maximization. To promote organic agriculture and to ensure fair practices in international trade of organic food, the Codex Alimentarius Commission, also framed certain guidelines for the production, processing, labelling and marketing of organically produced foods.

The popularity of organic farming is gradually increasing and now organic agriculture is practiced in almost all countries of the world and its share of agricultural land and farms is growing. As per a recent report of International Federation of Organic Agriculture Movements (IFOAM), the total organically managed area is more than 24 million hectares. Worldwide organic farming is practiced in approximately 130 countries and the area under organic management is continually growing.

There is a lot of debate between the proponents of organic farming and a section of the community who questioned the scientific validity and feasibility of organic farming. In intensive farming systems, organic agriculture decreases yield. The range depends on the intensity of external input used before conversion. In the Green Revolution areas (irrigated lands and well endowed water regions) conversion to organic agriculture usually leads to almost identical yields. In traditional rain fed agriculture (with low external inputs) organic agriculture has shown the potentials to increase yields. A number of studies have shown that under drought conditions crops in organic agriculture systems produce significantly and sustainably higher yields than comparable conventional agricultural crops often out-yielding conventional crops by 7-

90 percent. Others have shown that organic systems have less long-term yield variability. The organic farmers believe that much of the cases of suicides committed by farmers are due to the use of spurious fertilisers and pesticides which leads to crop failures. In such cases, the farmers are unable to pay back the loans and become debt-trapped. Therefore, the alternate way is to go for organic farming which is less expensive, environment friendly and ensures yields.

The factor productivity decreases as the soil is degraded due to excessive use of chemical fertilisers and pesticides. The crop productivity and production gets plateau after a certain level. But when the soil is restored back to health after use of different varieties of bio-fertilisers through organic farming, the crop productivity marks an increase. The productivity of sugarcane crop is found to increase by 25 percent through organic farming. Similarly, the productivity of some cereals and horticulture crops increases on account of organic farming. Besides, the consumers' world over have become conscious of organic food having no pesticide residues and the global market for organic food has grown to the tune of US$ 37 billion.

The common understanding is that large-scale conversion to organic agriculture would result in drastic reduction in world food supplies or large increases in conversion of undisturbed land to agriculture have not been borne out in modelling studies. Conversion studies showed that domestic food consumption would not suffer and exports would vary depending on crop but the structure of farming would definitely change with more diversification in agriculture. Widespread conversion to organic agriculture would result in crop yield increase over the current averages as a result of increased investment in research and extension. Organic farmers grow a variety of crops and maintain livestock in order to optimise use of nutrients and the space between species. This ensures economic advantages through low crop production or yield failure due to biotic and non-biotic factors in all of these simultaneously. This can have an important impact on local food security and resilience, should an unwanted phenomena happens. Livestock keeping at farms is an age-old practice. Livestock plays a major role in organic agriculture either as an intermediary between the utilization of crop residues or fodder produced at the farm and the return of nutrients as manure. Dairy in particular has helped number of small and marginal farmers to improve their income. Field survey has revealed that marginal and small farmers even in progressive states like Punjab have helped to raise farm profitability as well as availability of cattle dung in sufficient amounts.

Presently, only 30 percent of total cultivable areas in the country have irrigation facilities where agrochemicals use is higher compared to rain-fed zones. It is here that ingenuity and efforts are required to increase crop productivity and farm production despite recurrence of environmental constraints of drought and water scarcity. The basic requirement in organic farming is to increase input use efficiency at each step of the farm operations. Organic farms aim to optimise the crop productivity under a given set of farm conditions. There are ample evidences to show that agrochemical-based high input agriculture is not sustainable for long periods due to gradual decline in factor productivity with adverse impact on soil health and quality. Harnessing the varietal potential by appropriate biotechnology input is a neglected area and needs adequate attention.

The replacement of external inputs by farm-derived resources normally leads to a reduction in variable input costs under organic management. Expenditure on fertilizers and sprays is substantially lower than in conventional systems in almost all the cases. In a few cases, higher input costs due to the purchase of compost and other organic manure have been reported. Studies have shown that the common organic agricultural combination of lower input costs and favourable price premiums can offset reduced yields and make organic farms equally or often more profitable than the conventional farms.

Organic farming systems can deliver agronomic and environmental benefits both through structural changes and tactical management of farming systems. Some livestock farmers also find it difficult to justify conversion to organic production, due to high restructuring cost and lack of premium prices to compensate for yield reduction and also reduction in the area for organic production rotational constraints. Organic farming has been denigrated for being less efficient in land use and having lower yields than conventional farming and even accused of posing potential health risks. According to a commentary in *Nature* by Anthony Trewavas, Fellow of the United Kingdom Royal Society, "Although its supporters assert that organic agriculture is superior to other farming methods, the lack of scientific studies means that this claim cannot be substantiated".

The charge that organic farming is lower-yielding is misleading. Studies simply evaluating the reduction or elimination of inputs in conventional systems may not accurately represent conditions in alternative systems. Furthermore, abstract comparisons made when farms have just turned organic do not tell the whole story as it takes a few years for the yield to increase. Thus, it is necessary to make long-term comparisons.

The 21 year study found that soils nourished with manure were more fertile and produced more crops for a given input of nitrogen or other fertiliser. Nutrient input in the organic systems was 34 to 51 percent lower than in the conventional systems whereas mean crop yield was only 20 percent lower over 21 years, indicating an efficient production and use of resources. The ecological and efficiency gains more than made up for lower yields. In the long-term, the organic approach was commercially viable, producing more food with less energy and fewer resources.

The above overall information indicates that still there is a dilemma to agree on organic farming as a sustainable way of farming. Whether the small and marginal farmers are able to cope up with the sudden change in their income or not? A lot of studies are still going on all over the world relating to sustainability part of organic farming. By overlooking these literature reviews, we can decide that still there are a lot of misleading things which are unanswered. Hence, this study is being conducted to understand the real issues involved in the organic farming and to get the perception of other farmers.

Methodology

Objectives of the Study: Looking at various aspects of relation between climate change and sustainable organic farming, a study was required to understand the potentials and constraints in organic farming. More than this, to understand the strategies adopted by the farmers while shifting organic farming with the passage of time along with the state and economic policies towards organic agriculture, should be closely examined. There are various explicit and implicit factors related to this issue. With this backdrop, the objectives of my study had been stated more precisely as follows:

1. To study the potentials and constraints in organic farming.
2. To understand the farmers perception on organic farming.
3. To analyze the strategies adopted by the farmers while shifting to organic farming.
4. To understand the feasibility of organic farming in Odisha.

Data Collection Process and Sources: The study involves both formal and informal interaction with the individual organic as well as inorganic farmers; focused group discussion with the agricultural farmers and interview schedule for data collection. Both qualitative and quantitative data was obtained from different farmers.

Informal interactions with the staff of agricultural Department, village *sarpanch* and members of farmers' club helped us to understand the potentials and constraints of organic farming and getting further information regarding government policies for promoting organic way of agriculture for ensuring a sustainable livelihood.

Sampling Method: To understand the farmer's perception on organic farming and its feasibility in Odisha, the case study method has been adopted. Certain criteria such as size of land holding, from how long the farmer has been practicing organic farming and percentage of conversion into organic farming has also been taken into consideration which selecting the sample for study. In the present study, the primary data source has been given prime importance to understand the issues at micro level and as per people's perspective. Primary data source was also used to cross check the information gathered from secondary data sources.

For informal interactions and focused group discussions, no sampling techniques were applied. They were done with the available people at that time. The data collected was tabulated and used to draw inferences. No significance test was conducted. However, more importantly the intensive interview provided deep insights and these were used as reinforcements to conclusions.

Meaning and Sustainability of Organic Farming

Organic farming is a good and sustainable way of farming from all aspects like cost minimization, use of locally available resources and being labour intensive. Organic farming is one of the traditional farming practices. But because of Green Revolution in India, the inorganic farming was introduced and the same is developed till now. However, the trend of organic farming has started in India.

Organic farming may be called a sustainable way of farming because of its nature. Following components of organic farming explain how it is sustainable:

1. *Self-sustainability in seed management*: If the farmer is practicing organic farming, the crops that he has produced can be used for sowing purpose in the next crop season.

Here, the farmers need not purchase the seeds from market for sowing every time. It reduces the cost of seeds and reduces dependency on seed seller.

2. *Use of organic manure and bio-pesticides*: The bio-pesticides and organic manure can also be prepared in the farm itself. Here, the required materials are cow dung, agricultural wastes and other wastes that are decomposed by natural process. The use of waste material in and around the farm keeps the farm clean and it is of zero cost. Pesticide can be prepared by the farmer himself by using available materials like *neem* products, cow urine, curd milk, jiggery etc. This also does not need any cost for preparation. Beejamruta and Jeevamruta are two bio-pesticides which are approved by the scientists. The farmer himself can prepare these two bio-pesticides. The cost of preparation is also very less. These pesticides can be used for all variety of crops and for most of the diseases.
3. *Consumes less amount of water*: The organic farming requires less amount of water when compared to other farming practices. Use of artificial fertiliser or pesticide is not there in organic farming. So the use of water by the crops reduces. It results in less consumption of water and results in less exploitation of ground water.
4. *Fewer weeds*: Due to non-application of artificial fertiliser the weeds are very less. The requirement of labourers for weeding purpose is very less. It results in low cost of production. The removed weed can be used for preparation of bio-tonic by decomposing it with appropriate quantity of jaggary. According to scientists, the nutrients in this liquid tonic are very high when compared to all manures.
5. *Labour intensive*: The main concept in the organic farming is that most of the work is done manually. Here, the family members highly involve themselves in farming activities. That means that if the land size is small, the family members themselves can do all the activities. According to one interacted organic farmer, the application of external

labourers is reduced by 50 percent. But usually it is labour intensive, so the overall consumption of labour increases but the involvement of family members reduces the consumption of external labourers.

6. *Land fertility increases*: The use of organic manure leads to increase in the fertility of land. The nutrient content in the soil increases due to organic farming. The vermi in the soil will increase due to use of natural wastes as organic manure. It leads to sustainability in soil fertility. Here, the main thing is that non-use of artificial fertiliser and pesticides prevents the degradation of soil. Use of vermin compost and natural wastes leads to increase in the water content of soil and at the same time, the fertility also increases.
7. *Balancing the eco-system*: This is the main advantage of organic farming. Because of nature friendly farming practice, there will be a balance in the surrounding environment. The smoothness of the topsoil leads to increase in population of vermin. Decomposition processes will help the plants to grow faster.

Advantages and Disadvantages of Organic Farming

Advantages:

1. Low input cost: The organic farming practices results in low input cost. Overall expenditure on agriculture reduces drastically.
2. Nature friendly: The non-use of artificial fertiliser and pesticides and less consumption of water results in upgradation of natural habitat. It leads to environmental balance. Use of organic manure and vermi compost leads to increase of vermin in soil. It results in an increase in the fertility of soil.
3. Sustainable way of farming: Organic farming is one of the most sustainable ways of farming practice. Low costs and use of locally available resources leads to sustainability.

4. Less dependence on external factors: By case studies, it is proved that the dependency on external factors in organic farming is reduced significantly. The degree of dependency on external factors differs from farmer to farmer. But the dependency is reduced in almost all the areas from seed to manure.
5. Other benefits: Other benefits from organic farming are, farmer can produce compost manure and can sell. It gives an additional income to a farmer. Use of traditional varieties of seeds gives good fodder for cattle. It reduces certain amount of cost to the farmer for purchase of fodder for cattle.

Disadvantages:

1. Fewer yields: The overall yield in organic farming is less compared to yield that a farmer can get in inorganic way of farming. Because of low cost, the overall production budget of food grains is reduced.
2. Need for other income source in the initial stages: Due to very low yield, farmer's income reduces significantly. Hence, in that period, a farmer should find some other sources of income. But it is very difficult for small or marginal farmers because they may not have any surplus to invest in some other activities, which may yield income in that initial period.
3. Need to increase the overall production: It is necessary to increase yield in organic farming. The overall income is less. It affects the mass production process. If most of the people start organic farming, the production of food grains reduces, which will lead to a scarcity of food grains. Hence, we should look to improve yield of crops in organic farming.
4. Need to search newer markets for small farmers: Small farmers produce little amount of food grains but they really fail to market their products produced. Regarding organic farming, the yield itself reduces but the quality of product they produce is very good. They do not get good

price for their products. This area should be further explored. Suitable and accessible market should be created for their products.

5. Suitable for small farmers: Lot of arguments is still going on regarding the suitability of organic farming for small and marginal farmers. The yield reduces and need for other necessities required like supportive livestock etc. increases. Whether these groups of farmers are able to fulfill all these requirements is a big question. So it is still confusing that whether this farming suits small and marginal farmers.
6. Good government support: Now-a-days, the government is supporting organic farming. It is providing subsidies for organic manures and other incentives. But still it is a big question whether all incentives trickle down to the ultimate farmers. Most of the incentives are received by the big farmers only. Hence, it is a challenge to supply these technical incentives to small and marginal farmers to motivate them to practice organic farming.

Kaibalay Pradhan: A Case Study

Background of the Farmer: Kaibalay Pradhan is a well known farmer of the village Biakumutia under the Bansapal block of Keonjhar district of Odisha who has started organic way of cultivation for the last five years. He has five family members including two daughters and one son. He is leading a very happy life along with wife and children. In early days he was a teacher by his profession but had keen interest in agriculture as well as allied activities, although he had been doing agricultural farming of paddy, ginger and vegetables but was not doing it intensively. With the passage of time, the interest for agriculture goes up. He had left the job and started cultivation of his own. Kaibalay babu has five acres of cultivatable land along with two ponds for irrigation. There are six cattle including three milch jarsi cows which gave on an average ₹ 2,500 per month as an additional income. It says that practice makes a man perfect but I would say only proper practices makes a man perfect, what Kaibalya babu is now.

Table 6.1 Comparison between Organic Farming and Inorganic Farming Practices

Organic Farming	Inorganic Farming
• Traditional methods are used for ploughing • Less amount of seeds are required per acre • Old variety of seeds are used • Less amount of water required • Organic manure prepared by themselves no cost • Bio-pesticides like *Jeevamruta* and *Beejamruta* are used • Less weeds, less weeding process • Labour intensive-less labourers • Less input cost • Less output • High net profit • Nature friendly • Sustainable	• Modern instruments used • High seeds are required • Hybrid or GM seeds are used • More water required, exploitation of water sources • Artificial fertilizers are used • Artificial pesticides are used • More weeds, need more labour to remove weeds • Capital intensive • More input cost • Slightly high output • Less net profit • Not sustainable • Destroy ecosystem

Source: Field Survey.

Motivation Factors: Here, the factor that influenced the conversion is very important. Actually, any farmer will not wish to shift his cultivation process because he is familiar with the present way of farming and he is not ready to take any risk in his main livelihood practice, which will affect the major income source. Regarding the motivation factor, an NGO did a very well job here. PRADAN really motivated the farmers to shift their farming practice. In the year 2005, an executive of PRADAN visited the village to campaign in the village about the organic farming. The villagers and this farmer also did not believe the executive. But later the organization challenged the villagers and demonstrated the organic farming in the field of Mr. Kaibalay. PRADAN took one acre of dry land and cultivated ginger in organic way. The result was very good in the sense the yield was not so less but they got good fodder for the cattle. And the cost of production was also very less. By that Mr. Kaibalay changed his perception regarding organic way of cultivation and started to practice the organic farming.

Conversion Process: At present, has he converted his practice up to 90 percent. That means now 90 percent of the cultivation process is in organic way. He shifted gradually; in the first year he reduced his use of artificial fertilizer by 25 percent, in second year he reduced the use of fertilizers by 50 percent, and at present he has reduced the use of artificial fertilizers by 75 percent. In the same way, the use of labour was also reduced drastically. On the other hand, the yield of the crop was not reduced on a large scale because he shifted gradually in the sense that he is still using the artificial fertilizer in small quantities. If he had shifted immediately, the chances of low yield were there. But because agriculture being the main source of income, the NGO advised the farmers to shift gradually.

Other Farmers' Perceptions: Regarding the reaction of other farmers, some of them accepted and they are also now shifting to organic farming. But few have not accepted the new method but having seen the good result that the newly shifted farmers are getting in the form of low cost and high net profit, they are also shifting to organic farming. Here, we can say that the trend is going in favour of organic farming. The main reason why the few have not accepted it yet is due to low yield. However, they do not see the drastic reduction in input cost.

The farmer got the support from PRADAN in the form of technical guidance and in the form of marketing of the products produced by organic farming. At present, the government is supporting the organic farming by providing subsidies for organic manures. PRADAN suggested the farmers regarding the variety that can be used for sowing purpose. The main purpose of the NGO is to protect the traditional variety of crops because the traditional variety is very good from the point of nutrition, fodder for livestock and yield.

Crop Rotation: In dry land, he is practicing the crop rotation. One year he grows ginger and another year he grows pulses like groundnut or horse gram etc. Here, the crop rotation is mainly because of some benefit he is getting. If he grows ginger, the fertility of land reduces; so for next year he grows pulses, groundnut or horse gram etc. This is because the pulses like groundnut and horse gram receive the nutrition from the sunlight and they transfer such nutrition into the ground through its roots. In this way by the very nature itself, certain processes will take place which helps the farmer to grow various crops with good yield.

Use of Manure and Pesticides: After conversion into organic farming, the crops do not get any diseases. Ginger and pulses plants are not attacked by pests or any other diseases. Previously, ginger crop was attacked by a lot of pests and diseases. But after the conversion, the crops never got any diseases. The paddy is still getting small amount of fire disease and branch drilling pest attack. For that he is using kerosene. The kerosene will be spread to water in the paddy land, farmer will take a stick and will move the stick on the top of the paddy plant. The plants will dump in the kerosene mixed with water. By that the whole plant will take the kerosene. The pest will die or will move away from the field. This is the one of the traditional ways of controlling pest attacks.

The manure that the farmer used for production purposes was highly artificial and small amount of organic or cow dung manure was also used. Therefore, the input cost was very high and because of use of artificial manure, the weeds were also grown with high intensity and required lot of labourers and weedicides. But now, he is using more of cow dung manure and vermi compost which does not require any cost and also very less amount of artificial manure is utilized which is good for the yield. Hence, the cost of production has been reduced to a large extent. The transportation cost has also been reduced.

Role of Livestock: Livestock plays a very important role in the organic farming. From the ploughing to manure, most of the inputs are obtained from livestock only. The livestocks are used for all most all the activities in the farming practices. The farmer has six cattle. In that, three are giving milk.

Following are the some of the benefits they are getting out of livestock:

1. Milk for household purpose.
2. Cow dung for organic manure and for bio-gas.
3. The slurry out of bio-gas is used as an input to prepare organic manure.
4. Cows are used for ploughing purpose.
5. For harvesting purpose also the livestock are used.
6. The main advantage is the cow itself is it using for field purpose. There is no need of separate bulls for ploughing. Consequently, the consumption of fodder is also reduced.

Here, we can say that the role of livestock especially the cow, is very important from the point of organic farming.

Dependency on External Factors: The dependency on external factor is reduced to a large extent. The application of artificial fertilizers, pesticides, modern infrastructure and external labour is reduced significantly.

The main benefit that the farmer got is due to the reduction in above-mentioned input and cost of production is also reduced. From the point of farmers with small land holdings, it is really a good indication. But the dependency on livestock increased and the dependency on market for output has remained same. Interestingly, the farmer still practices the doorstep selling process.

Table 6.2: Changes in Dependency on Various Factors of Production

Factors of Production	Prior to 2007	In 2012
Seeds	The dependency is fully on market and the cost for seed was very high	The last year seed itself is used for this year sowing purpose
Tractors	Most tractors are used for ploughing purpose	Only cows are used for ploughing purpose
Labourers	More labourers are used for sowing and for weeding purpose	Reduction in weed resulted in less labour consumption
Fertilizers	300 kg. of fertilizers used for ginger, paddy and pulses cultivation	75 kg. of fertilizers are used for ginger, paddy and pulses cultivation
Pesticides	More diseases as above mentioned use of pesticides	Less or no diseases, bio pesticides are used
Nutrition in Food	Less nutritious food	Nutrition content in food is very high: no diseases to family members
Market Dependency	Dependency on market for output is very high	Now also dependency on market for output is very high
Crop Protection	The crop loss was very high due to various diseases	Crop protection is very high due to less or no pest attack and diseases
Soil and Water Management	Soil was degraded and water consumption was very high	Fertility of soil is increasing and consumption of water also reduced due to high moister content in soil
Information Sources	Only from Government Agri office	From Government Agri office and as well as most from PRADAN

Source: Field Survey.

The main problem to transport the crop is that quantity of output is very less. Compared to transportation cost, the doorstep selling is better (Tables 6.2 and 6.3).

Table 6.3: Expenditure Incurred for the Production of Ginger in 2012 (per acre)

Particular	Inorganic Farming (in ₹)	Organic Farming (in ₹)	Details
Seeds	1,80,000	0	6 Qnt. of ₹ 30 per kg.
Ploughing	1,500	1,500	₹ 150 per day of 10 days
Pesticides	6,000	1,500	
Compost	4,500	9,000	Per tractor 300
Harvesting	2,500	2,500	10 men of ₹ 150 each + 10 women of ₹ 100 each
Transportation to Separation Place	1,750	1,750	4 men of ₹ 150 each + 4 women of ₹ 100 each + 750 (tractor)
Cleaning Process	2,500	2,500	10 men of ₹ 150 each + 10 women of ₹ 100 each
Total Cost	1,98,750	18,750	
Earning	7,20,000	6,00,000	₹ 1,200 per Qnt.
Profit	5,21,250	5,81,250	Difference between earnings and total cost

Source: Field Survey.

Storage and Marketing: The harvested crops are stored in the ground. The farmer prepared a 5ft. x 5ft. x 5ft. step in the ground and side stones plaster it. It is closed at the top. The door is there at the top for the purpose of going inside to take the grains stored in the ground. The food grains are not affected by any insect. The marketing of the goods is not a problem. Sometimes the farmer sells some goods in the doorstep itself because of more transportation cost. The farmer is getting a good price for the products that he has produced in the land.

Benefits: The adoption of organic farming practice resulted in significant change in his field. First of all, the fertility of land increased and the moisture content in soil also increased. The farmer did not test the soil after conversion into organic farming. But because of his experience only, he understood that the soil fertility is increasing. The Green Foundation is helping the farmer to identify the increments in the soil fertility. The farmer is really getting good benefits because of irrigation facilities. He grows paddy with the help of irrigation. For mulberry and coconut trees also, irrigation facility is being used.

Conclusions

Agricultural developments in India need to focus on reducing green house gas emission through measures such as significant reduction of deforestation, improving conservation and management, effective restoring of land through controlled grazing, developing strategy that conserves soil, water resources by improving quality, availability and efficiency of use. While national network project, "Impact, Adaptability, Vulnerability of Indian agriculture to Climate Change" has been launched with a focus on impact of climate change on different sectors of agriculture production, it is necessary to make sufficient investment for adaptation, mitigation technology development, transfer and dissemination among farmers to combat climate change.

The need of the hour is to make an ecological transition to produce more food using fewer resources. This is possible only by adopting organic methods of farming. The success of our organic growers has shown that farm incomes can increase threefold by giving up the use of chemicals and by using inputs produced by on-farm biodiversity. It is irrational, irresponsible and unscientific to continue to destroy our vital resources and fragile ecological fabric of our planet through chemical farming and transgenic technology driven agriculture. Organic farmers face the same problems as conventional ones do. Unfortunately, organic farming takes a more integrative and more time consuming approach in resolving them. Considerably less private sector research support is allocated to organic farming.

References

Bhattacharya, P. and G. Chakraborty (2005), Current Status of Organic Farming in India and Other Countries, *Indian Journal of Fertilizers*, Vol. 1(9), December, pp. 111-123.

Kumar, K.S.K. (2007), Climate Change Studies in Indian Agriculture, *Economic and Political Weekly*, pp. 13-18.

Moharana, P.C. (2011), Potentials and Constraints of Organic Agriculture in India, *Kurukshetra*, pp. 20-21.

Pandey, Jitendra and Singh, Ashima (2012), Opportunities and Constraints in Organic Farming: An Indian Perspective, *Journal of Scientific Research*, BHU, Varanasi, Vol. 56, pp. 57-58.

Reedy, B. Suresh (2010), Organic Farming: Status, Issues and Prospects- A Review, *Agricultural Economics Research Review*, Vol. 23, pp. 350-351.

Thomas, K.V. (2011), Climate Change and Indian Agriculture, *Yojana*, pp. 16-17.

Vasudev, S.P. (2010), An Answer to Climate Change, *Kurukshetra*, pp. 35-37.

7

Climate Change Vulnerability and Livelihood Sustainability in Coastal Regions of India

Sibananda Senapati and Vijaya Gupta

Introduction

India has a nearly 8,000 kilometer long coastline that touches more than 60 districts in 9 coastal states. The two coasts (east and west) are different in many aspects, such as physical structure, economic activities, population and infrastructure. About one third of India's population live in coastal areas and the density of population is increasing at an alarming rate. The densely populated and low-lying coastal areas are exposed to frequent occurrence of cyclones, storms, and high rate of coastal environmental degradation. To add to these problems further, the change in climate is expected to increase the intensity of these events and also incite new hazards (e.g. SLR, extreme weather events like heavy rainfalls etc.) and new vulnerabilities with different spatial and socio-economic impacts. Historically, coastal zones are home to a large number of fishing communities. The well-being and livelihood of fishing communities is linked to the state of coastal ecosystems. Fishery is an important source of food, employment, income and foreign exchange in India. The coastal fishing communities have a traditional way of living. But the current pressure from urbanization is pushing them to poverty. Unregulated and over fishing along with the increase in fuel price puts tremendous pressure on coastal fisheries. The traditional fishermen are also restrained due to insufficient knowledge to adapt to the new fishery practices and change in environment. The livelihood of fisherman is therefore vulnerable both economically and socially to such changes. In this backdrop, the current paper discusses the vulnerability of fishing communities to climate change in India in general and fishing communities of Mumbai in particular.

Climate Change and Coastal Regions in India

More than 700 million rural and poor people in India directly depend upon climate sensitive sectors (agriculture, forest, fisheries) and natural resources (water, biodiversity, mangroves, coastal zones) for their subsistence and livelihood (Sathaye et al., 2006). A majority of the population earn their living in coastal areas through tourism or fishing. India has been identified by UNEP as one amongst 27 countries which are most vulnerable [1] to the impacts of global warming related accelerated sea level rise (SLR). The SLR is likely to result in loss of land due to submergence of coastal areas, inland extension of saline intrusion and ground water contamination and may have wide economic, cultural and ecological repercussions. Observations suggest that the sea level has risen at a rate of 2.5 mm. per year along the Indian coastline since 1950s. A mean SLR of between 15 and 38 cm. is projected by the mid-21st century along India's coast. Added to this, a 15 percent projected increase in intensity of tropical cyclones would significantly enhance the vulnerability of population living in cyclone prone coastal regions of India (Aggarwal and Lal, 2009).

Frequently occurring flooding and salt-water intrusion have direct effects on coastal agriculture, fisheries, aquaculture, freshwater resources, human settlements and tourism. The impact of climate change can also be related to the loss of biodiversity in coastal areas. The vulnerability atlas (BMTPC, 2006) of India shows 8.5 percent of total land in India being vulnerable to cyclones and 5 percent of land vulnerable to floods; 1 million houses are damaged annually. Between 1877-2005 a total of 283 cyclones (among those 106 severe cyclones) occurred in a 50 km. wide strip on the east coast whereas comparatively less severe cyclones occurred on the west coast (a total 35 cyclones). In 19 severe cyclonic storms, death toll was greater than 10,000. The super-cyclone of 1999 wreaked havoc in coastal Odisha claiming more than 30,000 human lives.

Similarly in July 2005, the city of Mumbai received an unprecedented 944 millimeters of rainfall in a 24-hour period, resulting in the most devastating floods in recent history leaving more than 500 people dead, mostly in slum settlements. While the vulnerability varies from region to region, a large part of the country is exposed to such natural hazards which often turn into disasters causing significant disruption of socio-economic life of the communities. Storm surges are also the major cause of coastal flooding along the east coast of India. The projected rise in the sea level may further affect the storm surges and consequently the coastal flooding in the east coast. The mangroves along the coastal regions of India including Andaman and Nicobar Islands act as barriers against cyclones, avoid coastal erosion and serve as a habitat for a number of aquatic lives specially fish, prawns and crabs. Climate changes will further disturb the delicate balance of the mangrove ecosystems and hence can bring out visible changes in them (Dash et al., 2007).

Coastal Fishing Communities in India

Coastal communities, here after referred as fishing communities, are living very close to the seas. These communities have quite different and unique relationship with the seas. They have been involved in fishing for generations. They possess a very distinct social, cultural, governance structure and traditional practices. In India, fishing communities have different castes depending upon their place of inhabitance. There are at least 2-3 castes in each coastal state, and they are exclusively involved in marine fishing and are not related to the mainstream agrarian system. According to Marine Fishery Census Survey (MFC, 2005), the total number of fishery population in India was 35,74,704 belonging to 7,64,868 families. A majority of them are active fishermen and rests are involved in fishing related activities.

Climate change has far reaching impacts on fishing communities. The projected climate change will directly affect the food security and livelihood of poor fishing communities. The high dependence on natural resources makes fishing communities particularly vulnerable to climate change. Climate change events like floods, cyclones, storms, heavy rainfalls often causes loss of human life as well as the loss of household productive assets (such as boats, nets, marketing facilities and jetties) in fishing communities. This is reflected in negative income effect in the capacity of fishermen as producers and leading to their reduced ability to earn income and sustain livelihoods. Fishermen are also less able to diversify their earnings because of their physical isolation which reduces their access to alternative livelihoods. Their income also varies as per seasons such as high income during good season and low income during bad season.

The past studies on climate variability, change and fisheries have mostly focused on deriving trends and fluctuations in fish stocks and distribution, particularly in relation to oceanic regime changes and the major pelagic [2] fish stocks of upwelling zones that are target of a large-scale industrial fisheries (Badjeck et al., 2010). It is found that the distributional and phonological changes of small pelagic fish and Indian mackerel may affect nature and value of fisheries. The small-scale fisheries in India will be the most vulnerable although most of the causes are attributed to the non-climatic factor. The sensitivity of this sub-sector to climate change threat is very high while adaptive capacity is low (CMFRI, 2011).

The study based on "indigenous technical knowledge (ITK) of fishermen on climate change" (CMFRI, 2010), shows that fishermen in the states of Maharashtra, Kerala, and Tamil Nadu have confusion regarding climate change and climate variability. They believe that the reduction in fish catch in recent years is mainly because of juvenile exploitation, habitat destruction and overfishing. They also believe that wind direction and wind speed are the two main drivers of fish abundance and availability, followed by rainfall and temperature. In most of the coastal villages, climate change causes an increase in salinity and higher tidal surges. There are many incidences of permanent submergence of land masses and increase in the vulnerability of communities and numerous impacts on the ecosystem and biodiversity. The highly populated areas such as the Ganga, Brahmaputra and Mahanadi rivers' basins are the most vulnerable regions in the country. Further, the rise in sea level will not only extend areas of salinity, but will also decrease freshwater availability in these areas. The CMFRI reported that about 75 coastal fishing villages of Maharashtra are located within 100 meters from the high tide line. The vector borne diseases like malaria and dengue are likely to persist in many states and new regions may become malaria prone and the duration of the malaria is likely to increase in many places of India.

Community Responses to Climate Change: The perceptions of fishing communities towards climate change, adaptation options, and coping strategies often varies among fishermen of different localities. However, it is important for them to understand the interaction between global change events and localized disturbances. According to Vivekanandan and Rao (2009), reduction of fish mortality that over-exploited over the years is the principal means of reducing the impacts of climate change on fisheries. Sustainable maximization of fishing yield through reduction in fishing effort helps adaptation of fish stocks and marine ecosystems to climate impacts. It also reduces the GHG emissions by fishing boats.

Most of the adaptation strategies of fishermen are intended to meet their immediate livelihood needs. For example, shift in fishing operations to catch several new varieties of fish species, decrease in the near shore fishing operations due to less availability of fishes, and increase in the offshore and deep sea fishing. There is also increase in fishing duration and fishing distances especially in fishing villages of Maharashtra and West Bengal. Fishermen are now fishing in a group of fifteen to twenty boats for the purpose of sea safety and exchange information on weather pattern and fish availability. The technological innovation such as the use of GPS, wireless communication, mobile phones helps fishermen in increasing their efficiency and reducing the time and operation costs (Salagrama, 2012). In order to balance the incomes, some boat owners operate with more than one boat.

Improvement in early warning system with the increase in number of television users and mobile phones often helps in providing better opportunities for getting information. The CMFRI, 2010 study also found that in the event of cyclones and sea erosion, fishermen of Tamil Nadu prefer temporary exit from their villages whereas the fishermen from Kerala prefer temporary exit as well as permanent rehabilitations to interior dwellings. A large majority of fishermen listen to and follow daily weather bulletins of the media. They are ready to take weather related insurance if the premium is within their capacity. Fishermen believe that fish catches will decline in future. However, they do not want to leave the profession, but want their children employed in government jobs.

Role of Government: Most of the climate change response measures in fishing are confined to the actions taken by local communities. Fishing in India is mostly treated in the same way as agricultural activities, although fishing communities have not yet received the required attention what agricultural farmers are getting. Considering the risk imposed due to climate change and the vulnerability of fishing communities, it is necessary that appropriate policy mechanisms must be in place to reduce the impacts. The policies for adaptation to climate change in fisheries should respond to existing vulnerabilities that exacerbate the impact of climate change, while enhancing resilience and adaptive capacity. Government policy must be developed to increase awareness on climate change among fishing communities as well as among decision-makers and managers and stakeholders in the fishing sector.

Coastal Regulation Zone (CRZ): Under the Environment (Protection) Act of 1986, the Ministry of Environment and Forests (MoEF), Government of India declared the entire coastal stretches as CRZ, regulating all activities within this area. Again in 1991, the MoEF issued an elaborate notification regarding CRZ which sought to regulate human activities in the area of 500 mts. from the high tide line (HTL) along the coastal stretches of the country. Four different categories of CRZ area are classified, such as CRZ-I (ecological sensitive), CRZ-II (built-up area), CRZ-III (rural area) and CRZ-IV (water area). Under the CRZ-IV, the above restrictions on the traditional fishing and allied activities undertaken by local communities are removed. In the last few years, the ministry has amended the CRZ notification many times. Recently in 2011, under the CRZ-IV, provisions are made to ensure livelihood security of the fishing communities and other local communities living in the coastal areas. Other major objectives of recent notification include conservation and protection of coastal stretches and promotion of sustainable development considering the dangers of natural hazards in the coastal areas and SLR due to global warming.

Deep Sea Fishing Policy: The deep sea fishing policy (1991) explored new possibilities towards enhancing the marine fish production in the country. The policy also facilitated greater inflow of foreign exchange through export of fish caught by the adoption of technologically developed foreign vessels. However, various other fishermen groups, mechanized fishing vessel owners, fish processors etc. heavily criticized the policy on the ground that operation of larger fishing vessels generates new problems like encroachment of traditional fishing area and fishing practices. Therefore, the new Marine Fishing Policy of 2004, emphasized on traditional and coastal fishermen in order to achieve harmonized development of marine fishery both in the territorial and extra-territorial waters of our country. The major objectives of this new marine policy, declared along with National Agriculture Policy (2004) were: (i) to augment marine fish production of the country up to the sustainable level so as to boost export of sea food and also to increase per capita fish protein intake of the masses, (ii) to ensure socio-economic security of the artisanal fishermen whose livelihood solely depends on this vocation, and (iii) to ensure sustainable development of marine fisheries with due concern for ecological integrity and bio-diversity (GoI, 2004).

Coastal Fishing Communities (Koli) of Mumbai: A Case Study

The research focus for this study is based upon coastal communities and to derive the socio-economic implications due to climate change on coastal communities. The study has been conducted in fishing villages of Mumbai. Being the financial capital, Mumbai is the most populous city in the country. The economic cost of climate change on Mumbai is huge. A substantial proportion of population in the city are fishing communities, popularly known as 'Kolis' living in Koliwada, and they happen to be the earliest inhabitants of the city.

However, recently their livelihood is affected by the extensive growth of the city. These people live very close to the sea, in small and overpopulated 'Katcha' houses. Kolis also bear most of the impacts of climate change.

Climate Change and Mumbai: The Canadian Climate centre's A2 (business as usual) and B2 (sustainable path) scenarios predict an average annual temperature increase of 1.75°C and 1.25°C, respectively by 2050 for Mumbai (Sherbinin et al., 2007). Similarly, an average annual decrease in precipitation of 2 percent is predicted for the A2 scenario and an increase of 2 percent for the B2 scenario whereas both the scenarios are predicted for a decrease in rainfall during

January to August and an increase in rainfall from September to November. Some of these changes have already been experienced as the city's temperature during March to May has been increasing over the years.

Similarly, change in the rainfall pattern is also persisting. Mumbai heavily depends on rainfall for the water supply and with the change in hydrological cycle the current problem of water shortage is going to be more intense for the years to come. Water shortage has always been a problem for Mumbai in the summer season. Many parts of the city face water cuts during this period. The SLR is predicted to be of 50 centimeters by 2050 for Mumbai. As mentioned earlier, Mumbai is one of the most vulnerable region to sea-level rise (GoI, 2012), a 1 meter SLR will cost ₹ 2,287 billon and will submerge 20 percent of city's land (TERI, 1996). The predicted sea level rise in the coastal areas of Mumbai along with storm surges will render the coast and low-lying areas uninhabitable where many squatter and fishing communities are located.

Flooding is a very common problem in Mumbai when heavy rainfall coincides with high tides or storm surges. Increase in rainfall and rise in the sea level along with the poor drainage system of the city will further increase the frequency and severity of floods. Climate models suggest that the hydrological cycle will be affected by climate change, with the intensity of heavy rainfall events rising and the number of rainy days falling (Challinor et al., 2006; Ranger et al., 2011). The failure of monsoon and change in rainfall pattern caused severe floods in the year 2002, 2005 and 2007. It has been observed that till 1989 the average rainfall of Mumbai was 2,129 mm.

However, in 2005-2006, the average annual rainfall was found to be of 3,214 mm (Kumar et al., 2008), an increase of 50 percent resulting the most devastating floods in recent history leaving more than 500 people dead, mostly in slum settlements. The estimated direct economic damage was more than ₹ 5,000 crores. There was no electricity in certain areas of Mumbai for five days. One million people were rendered homeless (Jenamani et al., 2006). The likelihood of 2005-like event is more than double and the extreme rainfalls could become more frequent. The low-income groups and poor residents living in vulnerable and low lying areas (accounting for nearly 50 percent of Mumbai's population) will be affected more.

Mumbai's Fishing/Koli Communities: The Koli communities are the oldest residents of Mumbai city. The word Koli refers to fishermen and includes a number of castes and groups. The fishing villages of Kolis are called Koliwada located along the coastline of Mumbai. According to the marine fishery census (MFC, 2005), there are 27 fishing villages and 5 fishing Talukas in Mumbai. The total Koli population in Mumbai is more than 50 thousand residing in more than 10 thousand families. The number of fishing villages in Mumbai is less in comparison to other districts of Maharashtra. However they are overcrowded. A majority of Koli communities in Mumbai are Hindus. There are also few Christian Kolis living in the villages like Worli, Mahim, and Madh. Table 7.1 provides the details of fishing villages of greater Mumbai region. Kolis of Mumbai are now at the crossroads, and their livelihood is at stake. A primary survey has been carried out in the fishing villages of Mumbai to understand the issues of economic, social and environmental changes on fishing communities. Some of the major issues are discussed as follows.

Over Fishing: There is an increase in the number of fishing boats due to government's financial support in the form of loans and subsidies. Increase in the number of fishing boats leading to overfishing coupled with the changing market dynamics, has put pressure on the fishing catch and its cycle (Salagrama, 2012).

Ecological Degradation and Pollution: Pollution of the coastal waters and the creeks from domestic and industrial wastes is another major problem for coastal fishers in Mumbai. Being the financial capital and major tourist destination, thousands of people every day come close to the coast of Mumbai. Some of the major pollutants of the sea water include sewage, chemical wastes and garbage especially plastic wastes, which often end up in the sea.

Table 7.1: Fishing Villages and Talukas of Greater Mumbai Region

District	Greater Mumbai	Total House-holds	Total Popu-lation	Persons Engaged in Fishing	Total No. of Fishing Boats
Taluk	Andheri				
Village	Madh	2085	10136	1681	676
	Versova	1079	5592	1457	564
Taluk	Bandra				
Village	Chimbai	56	336	93	61
Taluk	Boriwali				
Village	Charkop	17	72	0	0
	Erangel Bhatti	163	839	248	134
	Gorai	200	1205	232	150
	Malawani	575	2670	550	149
	Manori	357	2012	170	78
	Vazira	60	283	96	0
Taluk	Gr.Mumbai				
Village	Bandra	16	70	0	0
	Chira Bazar Chowpathy	18	84	8	8
	Colaba	300	1554	91	77
	Cuffe Parade	566	2738	362	254
	Juhu Tara	413	1857	353	43
	Kopar Khairane	92	547	127	80
	Maha.Jyothiba Market	7	41	0	0
	Mahim	1054	5114	202	127
	Mahul	250	1255	236	205

	Mandvi	25	135	0	0
	Mazagaon	70	341	22	1
	New ferry wharf	525	2714	38	0
	Sewri	115	571	67	5
	Sion	21	103	12	0
	Trombay	375	1542	375	169
	Vashi	73	389	110	104
	Worli	695	3453	598	261
Taluk	Khar				
	Khardanda	875	4422	1091	132

Source: Fish Production Report 2009-10, Government of Maharashtra.

Financial and Social Burdens: The entry of middle men and migrants into the fishing business has put a lot of financial pressure on fishermen. The Koli women, who were mostly in the marketing business, are gradually losing their traditional occupation. With the help of improved road and rail transport access and better refrigeration, fish dealers from far away places such as Odisha and West Bengal are now able to send their fish, even three days after a catch, to the Mumbai market. This has increased competition for the Kolis of Mumbai who continued to depend on fishing as a major source of employment and income. With the fishing business so badly affected, the Kolis do not go out to sea as frequently. Moreover, many Koli youth are not interested in the fishing business (Salagrama, 2012).

Climate Change and Koli Communities: Over the years the Koli communities have observed the changing weather patterns and climate. Now-a-days, there is huge difference in rain and wind pattern. Rainfall becomes more extreme, unpredictable—more often occurring in short, and intense spells. The monsoon comes a little later and ends earlier than its usual period. It now lasts for three months instead of the traditional four months; there is more rainfall in the later months of August and September than in the early period of June and July. With the increase in sea surface temperatures there are more stormy winds (particularly in October-November), stronger thunderstorms and lightning. Fishes which have a high commercial value are migrating to other regions and are going deeper into the sea seriously affecting the fishing business.

Survey Design and Sampling: This study is conducted based on pilot survey, secondary data analysis, and the discussions with various stakeholders (fishermen, government officials, and scientist from Marine Fisheries Research Institute). This study was conducted in five fishing villages viz., Versova, Madh, Khar, Mahim and Worli, located in the western part of the city. The villages were selected on the basis of population, households, people engaged in fishing and number of fishing boats. The pilot survey and in the later stage the primary survey was conducted in these villages through a structured questionnaire. The household survey was conducted over six months starting with the fishing season in the year 2011-12.

Sustainable Livelihood Approach (SLA): SLA has been very much useful in providing the likely impacts of climate change on fishery production systems and for measuring the potential impacts on the economic and social viability of fishery dependent households and communities (Badjeck et al., 2010). The approach deals with both the quantitative and qualitative elements. It is more useful at a local scale from individual, to household, to household cluster and to a village (Scoones, 1998). Besides, the SLA also addresses the issues of sensitivity and adaptive capacity to climate change. It brings together the critical factors, assets and activities that affect the vulnerability or strength of household strategies (Allison and Ellis, 2001). People and their access to assets are at the heart of livelihood approaches. The SLA approach considers five types of assets or capitals (human, natural, financial, social and physical) and uses multiple indicators to assess exposure to natural disasters and climate variability. These indicators include social and economic characteristics of households that affect their adaptive capacity, and current health, food, and water resource characteristics that determine their sensitivity to climate change impacts.

Further the SLA also provides the linkage between micro and macro issues, it brings together the resource users, local authorities and sometimes national policy makers to address a particular issue. The approach leads to a more holistic analysis of fisheries and climate change because it sees fisheries, not as a simple relationship between a community and an aquatic production system, but rather as part of a broader socio-economic system which is also affected by climate change. Climate change can be seen to impact each of the five types of assets as well as changing the vulnerability context and having impacts on policies, institutions and processes.

The survey questionnaire for the present study consists of ten sections that broadly reflect the five types of assets considered by SLA. These sections are: (i) households demographic information, (ii) occupation, migration and other characteristics, (iii) households physical assets, (iv) family income and expenditure, (v) borrowings and savings, (vi) climate change perceptions, (vii) marketing issues, (viii) health issues, (ix) other social issues and (x) adaptation measures.

Results and Discussions

The number of households surveyed was 200. After checking the validity and reliability of household responses to the survey, a sample of 182 households was selected for the analysis. Preliminary data analysis and results indicate that majority of the respondents (87 percent) were active fishermen and rest were engaged in marketing activities (mostly the female respondents). Out of 182 households, 164 (90 percent) had their own fishing boats, 53 (32 percent) had mechanized boats and they go for the deep sea fishing; in the peak fishing season (August to November) they make more than one trip per week. Among others, 96 (60 percent) had motorized boats and they do two to three trips in a week depending on fish availability. Motorized boats use dol nets and gill nets whereas mechanized boats use trawl nets and purse-seine nets. Rest 10 percent were daily fishermen and do fishing in nearby waters with their country made or traditional wooden boats. Majority of the respondents (65 percent) were young aged between 30-50, that is mainly because of the nuclear family system and their inability to shift to other jobs, 40 percent of the respondents had studied up to matriculation, as at a very early age they had to involve in fishing activities. The other reason towards this may be the government run schools in the villages which provide education up to 10th standard only. Table 7.2 shows utility and production services available to the households in the survey villages.

The availability of above facilities in the fishing villages has significant implications towards the livelihood of fishing communities. Being close to the sea, it is very difficult for fishing villages to get proper drinking water. The fishing villages surveyed in Mumbai are provided with such facilities by local municipalities; however sometimes they are charged towards that. Similarly, the existence of jetty and fish market facilities also helps in transaction of fish catch. Only two villages, Versova and Khar have jetty facilities whereas in Madh and Worli villages, demand for jetty and market facilities is long pending. Fishery co-operatives have an important role of intermediary between fishing villages and the local government towards the development of fishing villages. Fishermen are provided various financial helps in terms of loan schemes for building new boats or purchasing equipments, getting fuel subsidies, insurance etc. by the societies.

There are 35 fisheries co-operative societies in Mumbai, among those few societies are very active. It is found that 76 percent of the respondents have taken loan towards building their boats, 81 percent of them have taken loan through societies and only 40 percent have repaid their loan. The major reason of default towards repaying loan is their moderate income (53 percent of the respondents said that). The costs towards fuel, labour, transport, boat and net repairing etc. are continuously increasing along with the increase in the household expenditure like food, education, health, appliances etc.

Table 7.2: Utility and Production Facilities' Availability to the Households

	Versova	Madh	Khar	Mahim	Worli
Total Respondents	65 (36)	33 (18)	35 (19)	28 (15)	21 (12)
Electricity Facility at Home	Yes	Yes	Yes	Yes	Yes
Drinking Water Facility	Yes	Yes	Yes	Yes	Yes
Jetty Facility	Yes	No	Yes	No	No
Fish Market	Yes	No	Yes	Yes	No
Fishing Society	Yes	Yes	Yes	Yes	Yes

Note: Figures in brackets denotes percentage.
Source: Field Observation by the Author.

Further, the change in climate has put extra pressure on fishermen in terms of less availability of fish, fish availability at longer distances, less availability of high valued fish, damage to their house, boats, nets, health impact etc.

Perceptions of Fishermen on Impact of Climate Change: Respondents were asked to provide their ratings from very high to very low on observations regarding climate change (Table 7.3).

The Inter Governmental Panel on Climate Change (IPCC) has warned regarding the serious impacts of climate change on fish distribution. However, it is challenging to derive the relationship between climatic factors and fish production. One of the major problems in assessing the impact is the complexity of segregating the climate-induced changes in fish population from other human-induced changes in fishing (Vivekanandan, 2006). The records on fish catches are often influenced by economic factors such as the relative price paid for different types of fish. These non-climatic factors therefore over/under-estimate the climate related trends in fish catch. But there is no doubt that climatic changes will add to the problems in fisheries sector that is already characterized by stagnating catches, over utilization of resources and capacity and conflicts among fishers and many more reasons discussed above.

Table 7.3: Observations of Fishermen on Climate Change

	Very High	High	Moderate	Low	Very Low	Total
Rise in Temperature	67 (36.8)	82 (45.1)	21 (11.5)	12 (6.6)	0	182 (100)
Rise in Rainfall	44 (24.2)	57 (31.3)	54 (29.7)	27 (14.8)	0	182 (100)
Change in Rainfall Pattern	89 (48.9)	68 (37.4)	24 (13.2)	1 (.5)	0	182 (100)
Rise in Sea Level	22 (12.1)	78 (42.9)	52 (28.6)	28 (15.4)	2 (1.1)	182 (100)
Rise in Storm Heights and Frequency	32 (17.6)	78 (42.9)	53 (19.1)	19 (10.4)	0	182 (100)

Note: Figures in brackets denotes percentage.
Source: Field Survey of the Author.

Respondents were asked to rate the impact of climate change on their fish production activities (Table 7.4). The availability of fish in longer distances further affects the costs of fishing in terms of extra use of fuel and labour. Sometimes there is a drought-like situation (no fish production) for Kolis for which they demand compensation. Many of the city's local marine life is plummeting at an alarming rate and many species of fish like black spotted croakers (Ghol), bronze croakers (Koth), threadfin (Dara), perch (Karkara) and the Indian pike conger (Wam) are in danger of disappearing completely from Mumbai's waters. The worst-affected are the traditional fisher folk with small boats—over the years the catch per non-mechanized boats has been decreasing.

Table 7.4: Fishermen's Perceptions on Impact of Climate Change on Fish Availability

	Very High	High	Moderate	Low	Very Low	Total
Less Availability of Fish	101 (55.5)	67 (36.8)	14 (7.7)	0	0	182 (100)
Availability of Fish in a Different and Longer Distance	69 (37.9)	81 (44.5)	32 (17.6)	0	0	182 (100)
Less Availability of a Particular Fish	62 (34.1)	83 (45.6)	34 (18.7)	3 (1.6)	0	182 (100)
Loss of Fish Habitat	32 (17.6)	72 (39.6)	55 (30.2)	21 (11.5)	2 (1.1)	182 (100)
Loss of Coral Reefs	11 (6.0)	73 (40.1)	58 (31.9)	35 (19.2)	5 (2.7)	182 (100)

Note: Figures in brackets denotes percentage.
Source: Field Survey.

Besides climate change, respondents' perceptions on urbanization and its impact on fishing were also analysed. Mangrove destruction, water pollution, increase in construction activities often affect fishermen, especially small-scale fishermen who fish in nearby waters. Mangroves are the spawning and nursing grounds for a variety of fish. However, the large-scale destruction of mangroves and coastal wetlands (for real estate and infrastructure development) is another major reason for declining fish catch. Added to the problem, Kolis from the villages like Mahim, Bandra, Versova and Worli reported that a large proportion of the mass obstructing the water flows into the Arabian sea consists of polythene covers and plastic bottles, which are also the main 'catch' for any fisher attempting to fish in the nearby waters. The fish have gone further into the sea because of pollution (Table 7.5).

Table 7.5: Fishermen's Perception on Impacts of Urbanization

	Very High	High	Moderate	Low	Very low	Total
Mangroves Destruction	57 (31.3)	71 (39.0)	45 (24.7)	9 (4.9)	0	182 (100)
Water Pollution	111 (61.0)	61 (33.5)	7 (3.8)	3 (1.6)	0	182 (100)
Increase in Port Activities	12 (6.6)	52 (28.6)	52 (28.6)	55 (30.2)	11 (6.0)	182 (100)
Increase in Construction Activities	27 (14.8)	73 (40.1)	40 (22.0)	40 (22.0)	2 (1.1)	182 (100)

Note: Figures in brackets denotes percentage.
Source: Field Survey.

Conclusion

Climate change vulnerability studies, particularly for coastal communities, are very few because of the complexity of segregating the climate-induced changes in fish population from other anthropogenic changes. Therefore, this study has extensively dealt with the climate change issues pertaining to coastal ecosystem in general and coastal fishing communities in particular. Evidences from past climate change events as well as future projections show that the entire coast of India is vulnerable to SLR, coastal flooding, cyclones, storms etc. Coastal fishing communities depend heavily on coastal resources for their livelihood sustenance. The overpopulated and heavily polluted coastal regions along with the increase in urbanization and climate change has put additional burden on fishing communities and making their livelihood more risky.

This paper discusses all such issues along with various adaptation measures towards reducing climate change vulnerability undertaken by local communities as well as by the government. A primary case study of coastal fishing by "Koli" communities in five villages of Mumbai region was conducted. Fishermen's perception towards climate change, their adaptation measures, the government support etc. with the help of sustainable livelihood approach has also been analysed. The descriptive analysis shows that fishermen are perceiving and facing the climate change problems like rise in temperature, change in rainfall pattern which continuously affect their fish catch. Urbanization and pollution are also severely affecting the small-scale fishermen. The future scope for the study is to estimate the socio-economic impacts of climate change on fishermen and to develop vulnerability indicators at the household level.

End Notes

1. For detailed discussion on concepts like vulnerability, impact, exposure, sensitivity, adaptation, and mitigation, see Senapati and Gupta (2012).
2. Surface and sub-surface of the sea; inhabiting species living at the surface or in upper ocean waters, include tunas, anchovies and sardines.

References

Aggarwal, D. and Lal, M. (2008), Vulnerability of the Indian Coastline to Sea Level Rise, SURVAS (Flood Hazard Research Centre), available from; http://www.survas.mdx.ac.uk-/pdfs/3dikshas.pdf, accessed in October 2008.

Allison, E.H. and Ellis, F. (2001), The Livelihoods Approach and the Management of Small-scale Fisheries, *Marine Policy*, 25, pp. 377-388.

Badjeck, M.C., Allison, E.H., Halls, A.S. and Dulvy, N.K. (2010), Impacts of Climate Variability and Change on Fishery-based Livelihoods, *Marine Policy*, 34, pp. 375-383.

BMTPC, (2006), Vulnerability Atlas of India, Building Materials and Technology Promotion Council, Ministry of Housing and Urban Poverty Alleviation, Government of India.

Challinor, A. Slingo, J. Turner, A. and Wheeler, T. (2006), Indian Monsoon: Contribution to the Stern Review, HM-treasury.gov.uk., available from;

http://www.hmtreasury.gov.uk/d/Challinor_et_al.pdf, accessed in January 2011.

CMFRI, (2010) Central Marine Fishery Research Institute, Annual Report 2009-2010, Cochin, India.

CMFRI, (2011) Central Marine Fishery Research Institute, Annual Report 2009-2010, Cochin, India.

Dash, S.K., Jenamani, R.K., Kalsi, S.R. and Panda, S.K. (2007), Some Evidence of Climate Change in Twentieth Century India, *Climatic Change*, 85, pp. 299-321.

GoI (2004), Comprehensive Marine Fishing Policy Government of India, Ministry of Agriculture Department of Animal Husbandry and Dairying, New Delhi, India.

GoI (2012), Second National Communication to the United Nations Framework Convention on Climate Change, Ministry of Environment and Forests, Government of India, India.

Jenamani, R.K., Bhan, S.C. and Kalsi, S.R. (2006), Observational/Forecasting Aspects of the Meteorological Event that Caused a Record Highest Rainfall in Mumbai, *Current Science*, 90(10), pp. 1344-1362.

Kumar, R., Jawale, P. and Tandon, S. (2008), Economic Impact of Climate Change on Mumbai, India, *Regional Health Forum*, 12(1), pp. 38-42.

MFC (2005), Marine Fisheries Census 2005, Central Marine Fisheries Research Institute, Government of India, Cochin, India.

Ranade, S. (2008), The 'Kolis' of Mumbai at Crossroads: Religion, Business and Urbanisation in Cosmopolitan Bombay Today, in Proceedings of the 17th Biennial Conference of the Asian Studies Association of Australia, Melbourne, Australia.

Ranger, N., Hallegatte, S., Bhattacharya, S. Bachu, M. Priya, S. Dhore, K. Rafique, F. Mathur, P. Naville, N. Henriet, F. Herweijer, C. Pohit, S. and Corfee-Morlot, J. (2011), An Assessment of the Potential Impact of Climate Change on Flood Risk in Mumbai, *Climatic Change*, 104, pp.139-167.

Salagrama, V. (2012), Climate Change and Fisheries: Perspectives from Small-scale Fishing Communities in India on Measures to Protect Life and Livelihood, SAMUDRA Monograph, International Collective in Support of Fish workers, available from www.icsf.net, accessed in June 2012.

Sathaye, J., Shukla, P.R. and Ravindranath, N.H. (2006), Climate Change, Sustainable Development and India: Global and National Concerns, *Current Science*, 90(3), pp. 314-325.

Scoones, I. (1998), Sustainable Rural Livelihoods a Framework for Analysis, IDS Working Paper 72.

Sherbinin, A.D. Schiller, A. and Pulsipher, A. (2007), The Vulnerability of Global Cities to Climate Hazards, *Environment and Urbanization,* 19(1), pp. 39-64.

Senapati, S. and Gupta, V. (2012), Economics of Climate Change Mitigation and Adaptation: Moving from Impact Assessment to Vulnerability, *Interdisciplinary Environmental Review*, 13(2/3), pp. 105-117.

Vivekanandan, E. and Rao, G.S. (2009), Options for Adaptation, though Limited Exist, Marine Fisheries, The Hindu survey of Indian Agriculture.

8

Community Participation in Common Property Resource Management

Suman Devi and Nihar Ranjan Mishra

Introduction

Judicious use of common pool resources is necessary for a developing country like India. Their mismanagement has serious implication on both environment and the people. In India the common pool resources (CPRs) comprises of community pastures, community forests, village wastelands, watershed drainages, river or rivulet beds and banks etc. Within CPRs, some of them are owned by the Government agencies (Jodha, 1996). Watershed is a special kind of common pool resource (John Kerr, 2007). Indian watershed projects started in the 1970s and 1980s with technocratic approach that failed to recognize the need to address the challenges faced by the watershed projects. Subsequently, in 1990s, projects included participatory approach that focused more on social organization, but results remained vague (J. Kerr, 2002). However, much debate has been raised over local community involvement in managing CPRs. However, many successful watershed management programmes such as Ralegaon Sidhi, Adgaon (Maharashtra) and Sukhomajiri (Haryana), Jhabua (Madhya Pradesh) have shown that community participation is crucial to the success of these programmes.

Man and environment share a symbiotic relationship. These interactions leading to the conservation and management of common pool resources (CPRs) are conditioned by many social variables. Political, economic, cultural, technological and social factors play a significant role in this aspect. Traditionally, local communities used to manage CPRs. But, after India achieved Independence, the importance of decision-making powers at the village level has gradually declined. It caused damage to vegetation in rural areas and further led to deterioration in environment through soil degradation. Therefore, Government of India (GoI) and different local Governments took up various measures such as afforestation, soil conservation, run-off water utilization programmes etc., but failed to achieve long-term results from them (Reddy et al., 2004).

With the advent of modern capitalist industrial societies, CPRs which were once exploited for livelihood needs are increasingly being exploited for commercial gains all over the world. The impact of such indiscriminate exploitation of natural resources has created an acute scarcity of resources across the ecosystems of the world. While consumerism, urbanization, industrialization and overpopulation can be seen as man-made reasons for scarcity of CPRs, geographical variations across regions and natural calamities can be considered as the natural reasons. In this context, conservation and management of CPRs has gained significance across the world. Common pool resources are also called as common property resources; it could be either created by man or by natural processes (e.g. an irrigation system or fishing grounds etc.). There is difference between open access and common property resources; in open access property resources nobody has the legal rights to exclude anyone from using the resources. And in common property resources, there are defined groups who have legal rights to exclude non-members of that group from using the resources (Ciriacy-Wantrup, Bishop, 1975).

In economic terms, common property resources are defined as common pool goods. The common pool goods cannot exclude other users because of physical nature of the resource; on the other hand, the use of the resource by one user decreases the supply available to others. However, sometimes it is a misconception that CPR, managed by multiple users lead to overuse and degradation. There are mechanisms of defined rules and evolved norms for the regulation and conservation of shared resources for the resource users around the world. Most probably, overuse and degradation are largely associated with open access situations because the rights and obligations are non-existent or have been damaged by various pressures such as privatization and individualization, state appropriation, population increase, commercialization, or migration etc. (CAPRI, 2006).

Conservation in the context of CPRs can be defined as the management of human use of available resources so that it may yield the greatest sustainable benefits to present generation, while maintaining its potential to meet the needs and aspirations of future generations. Therefore, the concept of conservation of CPRs aims at preservation of the quality of our environment and ensuring continuous yield of useful materials—living or non-living—by establishing a balanced cycle of harvest and renewal.

Common property resources management is a wide area of study. To emphasize the role of community participation in CPRs, the paper deals with successful case studies of watershed management programmes with community participation in the Indian context. It tries to explore many dimensions of the CPRs and more particularly, dimensions of watershed management conditions which are responsible for the problems in managing CPRs.

Specific objectives of the paper are as under:

- To understand the concept of common property resource management, and
- To understand the role of community in watershed management programmes.

Sociological and anthropological tools and techniques have been used in the paper and the paper is based on personal field experience, available literature and reports.

Importance of Community Participation in Watershed Management

Watershed is an area from where all water drains to a common point. Watershed is an attractive unit for technical development to manage water and soil for production and conservation of natural resources (Kerr, 2002). During the past few decades, major policy changes have taken place in the area of natural resource management, shifting the focus from government agencies to user groups (Meinzen-Dick, 1999). People's participation is a process of bringing people into decision-making process in resource distribution or resource sharing. These people are those groups of individuals, who have been once excluded from the developmental process and further they are likely to emerge as the beneficiaries of the participation process (Chopra et al., 1989).

In watershed management programmes (WSMPs), involvement of user groups (UGs) refers to a meaningful responsibility and participation of user groups for resource management. Here, user groups monitor the use of resources and mutual consensus is formed among them for resource use. Sometimes, they involve themselves in watershed by making some investment on watershed structures such as farm pond, leveling of lands etc. on their lands. Community also participates voluntarily in planting trees or shrubs, cleaning the existing water bodies and cleaning roads and schools of the village. User group participation in watershed paves the way for effective participation of community in decision-making process. When communities themselves prepare the management plan, it creates a sense of ownership of resources among them and they successfully identify and solve practical problems related to management of watershed. Further, it ensures long-term support for better management planning.

In the area of natural resource management, the concept of integrated natural resource management (INRM) has evolved. Many countries have adopted this approach to protect the natural resources and agricultural productivity. It is also carried out with the community groups in some common property resources, open-access and privately owned resources, in micro-catchments. Similarly, watershed development programmes were also implemented with community participation in many developing countries by NGOs as project implementing agencies (PIA). Watershed has attracted the policy makers, as an effective device for poverty alleviation. Watershed fits into the sustainable livelihoods framework (Carney, 1998 cited by Lovell et al., 2003) which seeks to improve the lives of poor people and also support the sustainability of their livelihoods. People become aware of managing the complexity of rural livelihoods through holistic analysis of five capitals. These five capitals are, natural, physical, human, social and financial, upon which their livelihoods depend (Lovell et al., 2003).

Participatory Model of Watershed Management

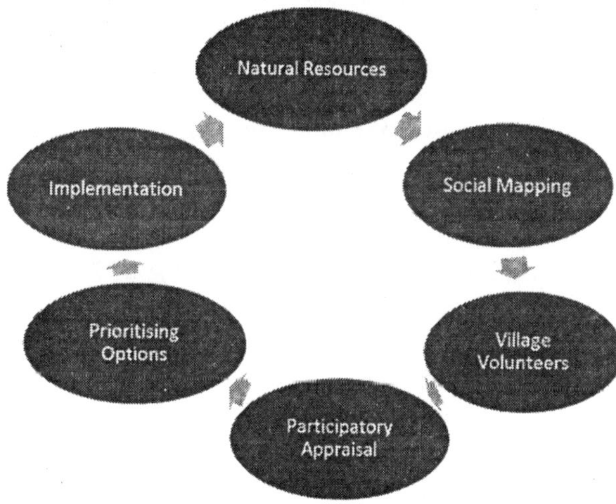

Source: Singh et al. (2002).

Watershed management improves the productivity of land, water and other natural resources. It is considered as the best means of CPR conservation along with other land and rural development programmes. CPRs generate employment and income for the rural poor and at the same time dominate the contribution made by other anti-poverty programmes in various areas. However, large scale privatization of CPRs has taken place during the last three decades (Jodha, 1986). The role of local communities in the management of natural resources/CPRs has been systematically reduced with increasing interference of the state, as the policy formulation and operational functions were delegated to the state employees. In the era of globalization, the state is challenged by international corporations and by citizens and communities. To deal with these new challenges, the state has often seen 'participation' as an input in mediating conflicts and relationships between its own administration, civil society and the private sector (Pimbert, 2004).

Therefore, more emphasis has been placed on the participatory approaches in natural resource management and more particularly on watershed management development programmes. The encouragement of community participation in watershed management is being initiated by international and state agencies with the belief that local communities who have knowledge and are close to natural resources should participate in management of these resources (Selfa et al., 2007).

Indian watershed projects started in the 1970s and 1980s with technocratic approach that failed to recognize the need to address the challenges faced by the watershed projects. Subsequently, in 1990s, projects included participatory approach that focused more on social organization, but results remained vague (J. Kerr, 2007).

In India, integrated and participatory watershed development and management has emerged as the cornerstone of rural development in the arid and semi-arid regions of the country. So far, substantial investment has been made in this regard. Till March 2005, approximately 45.48 million hectares have been treated under various watershed programmes with a basic investment of ₹ 17,037.42 crores; yet more ambitious plans have been made for the future. The Government has set a target of ₹ 76,000 crores for the next 25 years (Arya et al., 2007). The target of the watershed development programme is managing the natural resources in an efficient manner and intervening in the community development activities. People or communities are the ultimate beneficiaries of the programme. Hence, community participation is significant for the success of the programme.

Participation of the community in all programmes for rural development is considered as a pre-requisite to ensure their acceptance of the programme and its sustainability. Community participation is a complex concept having several meanings that change over a period of time. Sometimes, it could just mean a nominal membership in a group; and in other stages, it could imply having an effective voice in the decision-making process (Agarwal, 2001).

Successful Cases of Watershed Management in India Involving Community Participation

In the case of depleting natural resources and common property resources, laws and regulations are not sufficient for conservation. It is the people who can bring real change. Therefore, community participation carries extra weight in this regard. As we have seen, in many successful cases, community participation has brought remarkable changes in their lives and environmental management.

Case I: Ralegan Siddhi Village (Maharashtra): Watershed management is the process of creating and implementing procedures and programmes to sustain and increase watershed functions that influence plants, animals, and humans (Swami et al., 2011a). Taking rainwater harvesting as the basis, number of works have been carried out on watershed management in India. Organizations such as WOTR (Watershed Organization Trust), CMLR (Centre for

Management for Local Resources), Sehgal Foundation, TCSRD (Tata Chemical Society for Rural Development) are trying to handle the problem of water insufficiency through development of watersheds. Among many organizations and social activists, Anna Hazare et al. (1980) was the first in developing the Adarsha Gaon Scheme, which seeks to imitate Ralegan Siddhi Model in 300 villages (Maharastra state) with the collaboration of technical staff of Jal Sandharan program and social organizations.

The major factors for the successful people's participation in watershed management at the Ralegan Siddhi village are local leadership, imposing of moral sanctions for all, voluntary moral codes including restrictions on uncontrolled grazing and tree cutting etc., GO-NGO cooperation, participation of all sections of society, holistic and sustained development over long time (10-20 years), use of simple, proper and efficient technology for watershed management and dominance of village assembly in decision-making. But the limitation with this model of people's participation in watershed management is that, it is influenced by a strong and highly motivated local leader which is the fate of most of the Gandhian models of development. It is still to be seen if it is replicable when it is tested on the 300 proposed counties (Mishra et al., 1993; Swami et al., 2011b).

Along with the empowerment of people at grass root level, poverty is another most important development issue in India. It is estimated that 301.72 million Indians (27.5 percent) are living below the poverty line in 2004-2005. In the year 1975, among many states, Ralegan Siddhi was just another drought prone, poverty stricken village, but it has had much success in poverty reduction with community involvement in development process. But Ralegan Siddhi's success is not just a story of change as a result of access to water; but remarkable changes have been seen in economic, social and community regeneration also (Mehta and Satpathy, 2011).

The approach of project implementing agency (PIA) is different from location to location. In case of Ralegan Siddhi, the local leadership of Anna Hazare played a very important role to bring community together for the participation. He linked the development intervention with social set up of the community. He also developed feelings of group coercion and removed certain social evils. Apart from Ralegan Siddhi, other Indian states such as Sukhomajiri (Haryana), Jhabua (Madhya Pradesh) too have shown positive results of community participation in the success of watershed management programmes.

Case II: Jhabua District (Madhya Pradesh): The Bhill Adivasi (indigenous tribes of Jhabua District of Madhya Pradesh) traditionally managed water as a precious resource and used it judiciously. But water was commercialized by the financial institutions of the state. Financial institutions resorted to forced recovery of loans by the Bhills for lift irrigation in their area. This irrigation scheme failed due to faulty water management. Consequently, the tribes organized themselves (in the year 2006) to fight against this injustice. Finally, the Government of Madhya Pradesh responded to their demands, favoring the farmers. The tribe of the Madhya Pradesh has set up an example of mass political action and class for itself.

In the above case of Jhabua, it was almost a homogenous group. On the other hand, in other watershed areas, social heterogeneity in terms of caste and class plays an important role. Tribal people more or less have common interests, but in certain other cases, the groups may have different interests where collective action for management of CPRs in general and watershed in particular becomes difficult. Stakeholders differ in terms of their cultural background, interests and endowments (Bland and Platteau, 1996, cited by Ostrom, 2001), so they may act differently.

Case III: Sukhomajiri Watershed (Haryana): Sukhomajri, a village in Haryana's Panchkula district, became a model of self-reliant development during 1980s. It was highly affected by erosion problems near Shivalik hills. Upstream catchment area suffered from erosion problem and resulted in silting up of the downstream Sukhna Lake. Poverty and ecological degradation was high in this area. To deal with the problem, in the year 1977, Late Parasu Ram Mishra (a soil conservationist at the Central Soil and Water Conservation Research and Training Institute) and his team came forward. They constructed tanks to conserve rainwater. Villagers benefited by this stored water tanks and they used those tanks for irrigating the rain fed crops. This facility inspired them to stop cattle grazing and encouraged them to plant more trees. Farmers themselves protected their watershed in catchment in order to reduce the chances of erosion and stop sedimentation of their tanks.

Here, the problem of land ownership and landless people arose, because many graziers were landless so they did not need water and in no way they were getting benefitted. To solve this problem, all water was stored as a property of all villagers and landless people could sell their share of water to the landowner. The project was very helpful in enhancing livelihoods, improving agricultural productivity, reducing soil erosion, plantation of trees and joint forest management (JFM). The responsibility of management of dam and catchment was undertaken by hill resource management societies (HRMS) and HRMS were set up in scores of villages in the region.

Sukhomajiri model of participatory watershed management has shown constructive socio-economic and environmental benefits for all stakeholders. On the other hand, along with the role of farmers, the role played by Forest Division of Haryana (HFD) in institutionalizing a organization of water rights and managerial rules for management of water from earthen dams is of crucial importance (Kurian et al., 2005).

Problems of Community Participation in Watershed Management Program

Watershed management, although a technical intervention, is first and foremost a social process. In recent developmental programs, much emphasis was given to community-based approaches to environmental decision-making. In this regard, scientists must, more than ever before, should understand, appreciate, respect, and come close to local social set up. But formalization of the process of community-based management system does not ensure that local people will significantly consider scientific information and opinion when making decisions about watersheds (Rhoads et al., 1999). Community participation also depends on the household's socio-economic condition and its link with the livelihoods. The chances of participation are more by economically and socially well-off households than poor households. And people who are aware of government's decentralization policies are also more likely to participate in user groups created by regional officials (Agrawal, 2005).

Unequal distribution of benefits is another issue which discourages the community participation in watershed area. Many studies carried out in dry land areas on watershed development programmes declared significant improvement; mostly based on the optimistic biophysical indicators and new institutions built all through the projects. But so far, there is no realistic indication of equal distribution of benefits. Another factor to be considered is whether they have been successful in the eradication of poverty of most vulnerable sections (Srigiri, et al., 2003). Apart from socio-economic problems there is also a problem of knowledge exchange between project implementing agencies (PIA) and community. In many cases, the members of the community themselves have managed their watershed successfully. But sometimes over dependency of community on NGOs can be observed—it hinders the long-term sustainability factor, creates gaps in understanding technical aspects of watershed including hydrological problem, changing livelihood and land use patterns and upstream downstream linkages (Chauhan, 2010).

Ideally, external agencies (NGO, Government etc.) use the existing social network structures, norms and build trust with villagers in order to encourage them for collective action. But in practice, single purpose committees are most probably set up in communities where people are unemployed and they do not have many resources for successful collective action.

Finally, committees fail to generate the trust and reciprocity within a community. The causes behind this are lack of downward accountability and transparency. Adding to this problem, lack of proper coordination has led to unclear leadership (Vollan, 2012).

Local communities should be consulted in the design of development programmes. Otherwise, it results in failure of projects in achieving its targeted goals. Watershed projects are more efficient and effective when users are given a role in managing their own watershed resources (Johnson et al., 2001). But since the time of Hardin's work, "The Tragedy of the Commons" (1968), there has been a growing debate over common pool resources, property rights, and resource depletion. The article explained the problem of overexploitation of forests and fisheries, overgrazing, air and water pollution, misuse of public lands, population, extinction of species, and how unequal distribution of resources among community members led to a 'tragedy' (Stevenson, 1991, cited by Adhikari, 2001).

The management of CPRs can be regarded as a problem of collective action, analyzed in terms of the costs and benefits of coordination, institutional development and maintenance. It is done according to variables such as group size, composition, relationship with external powers, and resource characteristics (Adams et al., 2003). Best example for these types of assumptions is a case study from Asia and Sub-Saharan Africa. In the 1970s and 1980s, the governments and donors agencies have faced the problem of fuel wood crisis in these countries. To solve this problem, they developed social forestry projects to influence smallholders to plant trees on their farmlands. On the contrary, research in these areas has shown that these interventions were not effective.

Some of the households positively planted trees to provide fuel. But many others solved the problem of scarcity by sharing cooking arrangements, growing labor devoted to collection, substituting between fuels, migrating or engaging in nomadism and transhumance. And the farmers who have planted trees primarily did it for commercial gain not as a substitute for fuel wood. Here, it can be analyzed that there is gap between the perception of problem of wood scarcity between the government planners/donors and that of small farmers. And it supports the idea that, there is no clarity between government and local communities over objectives and approach to solve the problem of scarcity (Arnold, 1997, Leach, 1998, Adams et al., 2003).

But this case cannot be generalized because the management of common pool resources is highly dependent on the type of resource involved. An innovative strategy at one location or of one particular resource may not be necessarily applicable to others (Ostrom, 2001). To deal with challenge of common pool resources, Ostrom proposes the solution of 'adaptive governance' as a technique for the management of CPRs. Adaptive governance is appropriate for solving the problems that are complex, uncertain and fragmented. Ostrom (2001) outlines five basic requirements for achieving adaptive governance, which are as follows:

- Achieving accurate and relevant information with the help of scientific knowledge used by both the managers and the users of the resource.
- Dealing with conflict and devise mechanisms to discover it and resolve it within very short span of time.
- Enhancing rule compliance by creating responsibility for the users of a resource to guide the usage.
- Providing infrastructure that is flexible over time, both to aid internal operations and create links to other regimes.
- Encouraging adaption and change to deal with errors and adjust with new situations.

It is possible that decision-makers and stakeholders are different in their access, understanding and knowledge. Therefore, the knowledge of any particular stakeholder is not complete and hence it may be contested by other actors. A deeper understanding of stakeholder differences over CPRs may solve the problem to some extent but it does not guarantee that policy negotiations will result in win-win situations. But it may result in harmonious conditions, if there are incompatibilities in stakeholders' interests, values, and priorities (Hess and Ostrom, 2001).

Sometimes, the empirical facts on management of CPRs suggest a more complex situation. There are number of examples of resource problems, from the difficulties in achieving international agreement on the Kyoto Protocol to the cases of the 'collapse' of societies that failed to manage common resources (Jared Diamond, 2000 for the collapse of the Mayan civilization and other striking cases). But there are also cases where local societies have effectively managed common property resources, some of them even without the government intervention (Walton, 2008).

Conclusion

In this paper, theories on common pool resource management have been used to study the dimensions and problems of CPRs in many situations. Theoretical backgrounds have also been presented in the paper. Some of them believe that CPRs are best managed by local communities. On the other hand, some of researchers, policy makers, and environmentalist are of the opinion that there is need for outsider's intervention (Hardin, 1968; Steward, 1994; Wittfoget, 1957). But community involvement largely depends on community's needs, dependency, awareness, approach of external agencies, and socio-economic environment etc.

Apart from this (Ostrom, 1990), has given very balanced opinion. She is of the view that, choice of a management system depends on the situation-specific factors. And (Olson,

1965) gave a very optimistic idea of managing common pool resources in terms of collective action in the context of small groups.

In watershed situation, face to face and regular interaction between beneficiaries and PIAs may resolve various issues related to watershed maintenance during project and post-project period. Undistorted communication should be ensured and defined roles for each of project receivers to maintain the water harvesting structures and other assets created by the WSDP should exist. In this paper, it was found that community as an independent variable controls the other dependent variable. For example, if the farmer is poor and landless, his participation is generally low in watershed meetings and decision-making.

Further, daily wage labor is not a sustainable activity in these areas as daily wage laborers lose their livelihood during the post-project period. Good micro finance arrangements are necessary and they should be properly invested by the beneficiary. Further research and policy changes are needed in CPRs which can be generalized and used in all situations and particularly in the field of watershed management. The policy must follow some flexible approach suited to the real situation. For example, investment on various watershed structures could be changed if needed by the farmers. In some cases, it was observed that some of the PIAs do not fulfill the primary needs of communities such as livelihood, drinking water etc., and it leads to the loss of interest in the local community for participation.

A working institutional arrangement at national, state, district and block level is already in place to ensure cooperation with each other legitimately. Apart from this, village community must create a small group within each locality to share their experience to manage the watershed resources more effectively. Further, for any help they should approach the *gram panchayat* (GP) and in turn the GP must be cooperative and productive. Therefore, overall linking of all institutions is required to make the programme more fruitful and for this, community has to be more active. Ostrom's (2001) model of 'adaptive governance' may also be effective in watershed management programme. For sustainability of the programme, permanent sources of livelihoods and regular community mobilization in post-project period is needed.

References

Adhikari, B. (2001), Literature Review on the Economics of Common Property Resources: Review of Common Pool Resource Management in Tanzania, Centre for Ecology, Law and Policy Environment Department, University of York, Report Prepared for NRSP Project R7857.

Aggrawal, R.M. (2006), Globalization, Local Ecosystems, and the Rural Poor, *World Development,* Elsevier Ltd., Vol. 34, No. 8, pp. 1405-1418.

Agrawal, Arun and Gupta, Krishna (2005), Decentralization and Participation: The Governance of Common Pool Resources in Nepal's Terai, *World Development*, Vol. 33, Issue 7, pp. 1101-1114.

Hess, C. Ostrom, (2001), Artifacts, Facilities and Content: Information as a Common Pool Resource, Conference on the Public Domain, Duke Law School, Durham, North Carolina, November 9-11.

Jodha, N.S. (1986), Common Property Resources and Rural Poor in Dry Regions of India, *Economic and Political Weekly* , Vol. 21, No. 27, pp. 1169-1181.

Johnson, N., Ravnborg, H.M., Westerman, O. and Probst, K. (2001), Participation in Watershed Management and Research, CAPRI, IFPRI, Paper No.19, Washington D.C.

Kerr, J. (2002), Watershed Development, Environmental Services, and Poverty Alleviation in India, *World Development*, Elsevier Science Ltd., Vol. 30, No. 8, pp. 1387-1400.

Kerr, J. (2007), Watershed Management: Lessons from Common Property Theory, *International Journal of the Commons,* Utrecht Publishing and Archiving Services for IASC, Vol. 1, No. 1, pp. 89-109.

Kerr, John (2002), Watershed Development, Environmental Services, and Poverty Alleviation in India, *World Development*, Elsevier Science Ltd., Vol. 30, No. 8, pp. 1387-1400.

Kurian, Mathew and Dietz, Tone (2007), Hydro-Logic: Poverty, Heterogeneity and Cooperation on the Commons, MacMillan.

Kurian, Mathew and Dietz, T. (2005), How Pro-poor are Participating in Watershed Management Projects? An Indian Case Study', Colombo, Sri Lanka: International Water Management Institute (IWMI), (IWMI Research Report 92).

Leach, M. Mearns and M. Scoons (1999), Environmental Entitlements: Dynamics and Institutions in Community-Based Natural Resource Management, *World Development*, Elsevier Science Ltd., Vol. 27, No. 2, pp. 225-247.

Mishra, B. (1993), Successful Case of Participatory Watershed Management at Ralegan Siddhi Village in district Ahmednagar, Maharastra, India, Association of Voluntary Agencies for Rural Development (AVARD), New Delhi.

Mehta, A., K., Satpathy, T. (2001), Escaping Poverty: The Ralegan Siddhi Case, Indian Institute of Public Administration, New Delhi.

Margaret, A.M., Ostrom, E. and Gibson, C. (2000), People and Forests: Communities, Institutions, and Governance [Online], MIT Press, Cambridge, London, available from http://books.google.co.in/, accessed on 2nd December 2012.

Mark, Lubell, Mark Schneider and John T. Scholz (2002), Watershed Partnerships and the Emergence of Collective Action, *American Journal of Political Science*, Vol. 46, No. 1 pp. 148-163.

Ostrom, E., Richard B. Norgaard and David Policansky (2001), Reformulating the Commons, Burger, J. Ostrom, E. Norgaard, E. Policansky and B.D. Goldstein (eds.), Protecting the Commons: A Framework for Resource Management in the Americas, [Online], Island Press, available from http://books.google.co.in/, accessed on 2nd December 2012.

Pimbert, M. (2004), Institutionalizing Participation and People-Centered Processes in Natural Resource Management: Research and Publications Highlights, International Institute for Environment and Development (IIED), Institute of Development Studies, Vol. 3, United Kingdom.

Pretty, J. and Ward, H. (2001), Social Capital and the Environment, *World Development*, Elsevier Science Ltd., Vol. 29, No. 2, pp. 209-227.

Peter, A.C. and Nielsen, E. (2001), Indigenous People and Co-management: Implications for Conflict Management, *Environmental Science and Policy*, Vol. 4, pp. 229-239.

Reddy, Y.V.R., G. Sastry, B. Hemlatha, Om Prakash and Y.S. Ramakrishna (2004), Evaluation of Watershed Development Programmes in India, ISCO, 13th International Soil Conservation Organization Conference, Brisbane, July.

Rhoad, Brucel, Wilson, David and Herrics, Edwin E. (1999), Interaction between Scientists and Nonscientists in Community-Based Watershed Management: Emergence of the Concept of Stream Naturalization, *Environmental Management*, Vol. 24, No. 3, pp. 297-308.

Swami, V., Kulkarni, S.S., Kumbhar, S. and Kumbhar, V. (2012), Participatory Watershed Management in South Asia: A Comparative Evaluation with Special References to India, *International Journal of Scientific and Engineering Research*, Vol. 3, Issue 3, March.

S. Reddy, Srigiri, R. Chennamaneni and K. Hagedorn (2003), Equity and Poverty Issues in Watershed Development Projects-A Case Study of Impact Assessment on Marginal Farmers and Landeless, Conference on International Agricultural Research for Development, Deutscher Gottingen, October 8-9.

Wantrup, C. Siegfried and V. Richard, C. (1975), Common Property as a Concept in Natural Resource Policy, *Natural Resources Journal*, Vol. 15, pp. 713-727.

Walton, M. (2008), Managing Common Property Resources, Forest and Pasture Management in Colombia and Rajasthan, Course 902, *Issues in Economic Systems and Institutions*, Delhi School of Economics, Department of Economics, University of Delhi.

9

Joint Forest Management and Sustainable Rural Livelihoods

Raghunath Sahoo and Mamata Swain

Introduction

In a developing economy like India, the development of rural economy through effective and proper management of common property resources (CPRs) such as forests has increasingly become an integral part of sustainable development policy in the past couple of decades. This policy initiative has become popular due to strong disillusionment with the performance of central management policy to provide sufficient incentives to the users to manage CPRs in a sustainable way. Some researchers (Jodha, 1986; Wade, R. 1987; Chopra et al., 1990) found that the well organized community-based institutions can play a significant role in overcoming the socio-economic problems faced by the rural economy and can avoid the tragedy of commons as envisaged by Hardin (1968). In this context, an identification and preservation of community-based forest resources through granting community property rights over local natural resources deserves serious concerns in so far as they can be highlighted as an instrument to enhance poverty alleviation, environmental conservation and economic development.

The recognition of community-based forest has led to the devolution of forest resource management from centralized to local level user groups in India (Behera, 2006). In fact, Government of India adopted a participatory approach in management, protection and development of forest resources under the aegis of joint forest management (JFM) that was introduced in the National Forest Policy of 1988 followed by June 1990 circular issued by the Government of India in this regard. Till date, almost 22 states have issued requisite orders to facilitate implementation of the JFM and elicit people's participation in managing the forest resources.

JFM is a policy based programme, which seeks to establish management 'partnerships' between village forest dependent communities and the state for the sustainable management and benefit sharing of forest. With the introduction of joint forest management (JFM) in the 1990s, a policy sought the involvement of village communities and voluntary agencies in the regeneration of degraded forest land. Under JFM, the forest department (mostly a local forest official as the secretary of the committee) and the village community enter into an agreement to constitute a committee to jointly protect and manage the village forest. The key understanding in the arrangement is that in return for protecting forest land and helping in the regeneration and management of the said forest, people will be entitled to usufruct rights over dead fuelwood, timber, NTFPs as well as a significant share ranging between 25 to 50 percent (it varies from state to state) of timbers (in cash or kind) on final harvesting. But the community and the forest department are expected to share not just the benefits, but the responsibilities too.

In other words, JFM strategies bring local forest users, NGOs and the forest department onto a common platform for the management of forests. The institutional framework and the procedure of operation, to a certain extent, vary from state to state as each state has issued its own JFM resolution. The JFM programme, over the past decade, has spread all over the country. The area under JFM is now 17,331,955.12 hectare involving 84,632 groups (India State of Forest Report, Government of India, 2009).

Joint forest management (JFM) was introduced in Odisha on 1st June 1988 by JFM resolution and subsequently into other states like West Bengal, Bihar, Gujarat, Rajasthan, Andhra Pradesh, Madhya Pradesh, and Karnataka. This is a co-operative experiment where the foresters, NGOs and the local communities are involved in the protection, regeneration of degraded forest land and management of resources. The stakeholders are ensured property rights in the management of forest resources under the system of JFM. Under this policy initiative, the degraded national forests were handed over to the forest protection committees (FPCs) as community forest under a community-based property rights regime. In response to the national forest policy and to ensure equity and social justice, the state governments, which are responsible for forest management under Indian constitution, have started encouraging the communities living near the state forests for formation of forest protection committees (FPCs) under JFM.

With regard to implementation of the new forest policy, a comparative analysis among the states of India shows that a poor and tribal dominated state like Odisha, which is located in the eastern part of India, is the first state to introduce the participatory approach in forest management by forming a number of FPCs in a bid to revive the degraded forest resources in the early 1990s. Till date, Odisha has the largest FPCs among all the Indian states. Forest protection committee (FPC) is constituted for this purpose by the Divisional Forest Office (DFO). The members will be selected from the concerned villages; the villagers will get 25 percent of benefits and can collect all the fallen twigs, grass, fruits, flowers, seeds (excluding cashew) and leaves. Though JFM gives back some of the original rights to the local communities, it still retains the power centre with the forest department.

In this study, an attempt has been made to examine the outcome of participatory approach, the relationship among poor and non-poor households and access to and benefits from community-based forest resource management under joint forest management (JFM) in Odisha. In order to examine such relationship, a field investigation was undertaken among 200 sample households from four villages in Keonjhar district of Odisha. The household level benefits were estimated in terms of employment opportunities, income from small timber and non-timber forest products (NTFPs), and fuel wood collection for own consumption and sale from the forest under JFM.

Review of Literature

Poverty, property rights and people's participation on the management of CPRs are increasingly becoming a major subject of debate, discussions and investigations, particularly on the issues of local collective actions or community-based natural resource management over the past couple of years. One group of researchers advocate that common property resource users can create and sustain the local level institutions that ensure equitable access to, and income from resource management. Furthermore, CPR literature claims that poor people are more dependent on natural resources; they derive higher income and benefits from CPRs. Some researchers, on the other hand, advocate that compared to the non-poor, the poor people may depend more on common resources, but in absolute terms their dependency is lower. Thus, the problems and policies on the participation of local people and institutions on the management of CPRs deserve serious concern in the various studies undertaken by different scholars over the years.

Anderson (1995) found that wealthy and influential villagers in the control of forest councils use these resources for their personal use and poor do not gain from this JFM. A study based on the 180 households in 20 villages of Andhra Pradesh found that the rich households get larger chunk of income from the commercial exploitation of NTFPs by influencing the decision of the FPCs in their favour. In a similar study, Hill and Shields (1998) observed pertaining to 130 households in Andhra Pradesh, Madhya Pradesh and Rajastan that the main losers in the JFM are fuelwood loaders who are often the poorest sub-group within the village studied.

Kumar (2002) found that in his studies on six villages of Ranchi district of Jharkhand the rich who gain under joint forest management (JFM) is more than the poor who are the net losers in this process by using cost-benefit analysis.

A study of Van Panchayats in Uttar Pradesh (U.P.) by Ballabh, V. and Singh, K. (1988) have found that informal management by the people may have prevailed in the distant past but it disappeared in the wake of the British take over. Van Panchayats which were constituted in U.P. since about 1930s can be considered as an attempt to revive people's participation. In 1985 as many as 4,058 of them existed in the state. Most of them could effectively prevent encroachment through informal measures, but encroachment did occur in few cases. They have also been fairly effective in regulating resource use to prevent unsustainable exploitation. In a study of two districts of Nepal, Adhikari (2002) identified that the poor stake holders are currently benefitting less in terms of average annual gross and net income from community forestry than the relatively better off households.

Rath and Sahu (2004) have also identified in a poor state like Odisha that there is a good scope for harnessing of CPRs in Odisha. They found that proper utilization of CPRs would bring improvements in the standard of living of the people, particularly the poor and landless labourers and tribals in terms of increased employment and income generation from them. They have also studied that the success of rural development policy depends on the people's participation and stakeholders should be granted more management rights over the CPRs, more particularly in the rural areas.

Study Area, Methodology and Data Collection

India, the second highest populated country of the world, inhabits about 16.08 percent of the total world population with 2.47 percent of world's landmass and about 7 percent of world's forest area. As per the India State of Forest Report, 2009, the total forest cover of the country (2007 assessment) is

690,899 sq. km. and this constitutes 21.02 percent of the geographical area of the country. Of this, 83,510 sq. km. (2.54 percent) is very dense forest; 319,012 sq. km. (9.71 per cent) is moderately dense forest, while 289,377 sq. km. (8.77 percent) is open forest cover. An examination of the forest coverage area of major states in India reveals that the state of Odisha is well endowed with forest resources in comparison to other major states of India. Odisha, the fifth largest state in terms of forest coverage area is 48,855 sq. km. in India, which accounts for 7.07 percent of the total forest area of the country. Madhya Pradesh accounts for the largest forest cover of the country (11.24 percent), followed by Arunchal Pradesh (9.74 percent), Chhatisgarh (8.08 percent), Maharashtra (7.33 percent), and Andhra Pradesh (6.53 percent).

Though the forest area in the state during 1998-99 was 58,135 sq. km., which constitutes 37.34 percent of the total geographical area of the state, it had declined over the years. As per the *State Forest Report, 2009*, the state has only 48,855 sq. km. of forest cover, i.e., 31.38 percent of the total geographical area of the state. Further, the grouping of the forest area into different components shows that 7,703 sq. km. (15.76 percent) is very dense forest, 21,394 sq. km. (43.79 percent) is moderately dense forest and 20,388 sq. km. (47.13 percent) is open forest. In fact, the recorded forest area is 58,136 sq. km. which constitutes 37.34 percent of the total geographical area of the state. Of this, 26,329 sq. km. (45.28 percent) is reserved forests; 15,525 sq. km. (26.70 percent) is protected forests, while 16,282 sq. km. (28 percent) is unclassified forests cover. The total protected and unclassified forest land is 31,807 sq. km., which constitutes 51.71 percent of the total recorded forest area on CPR forest land.

One of the salient features of the National Forest Policy is to associate people actively in the protection, conservation and management of forests. The National Forest Policy stipulates that 33 percent of the geographical area should be under forest cover. With a view to enhance the forest coverage area, the

State government has initiated many measures with the provisions made by the National Forest Policy of 1988. It has promoted Village Forest Committees (VFCs), Village Forest Protection Committees (VFPCs), Vana Samrankhyan Samities (VSSs) in different districts of the state. Village Forest Committees (VFCs) were formed under Odisha Forest Rules, 1985. Forest Protection Committees (FPCs) were formed under the National Forest Policy of 1988 and Vana Samrankhyan Samities (VSSs) were formed under 1993 and 1996 resolutions.

Apart from these, there are several unregistered committees functioning simultaneously. There were about 1,199 JFM committees in 2005, managing around 14 percent forest area. Nearly 17 million families were involved in this programme of which around 0.7 million families belonged to tribal communities. By the end of 2010-11, 11,915 Vana Samrankhyan Samities (VSSs) and 398 Eco-Development Committees (EDCs) were formed in the state for protecting and regenerating forest areas of around 11,238 sq. km. of forest area for protection through joint forest management approach and around 11,428 families were members of these VSSs and EDCs (Economic Survey, 2011, Government of Odisha).

After the joint forest management (JFM) resolution implemented by the state government, so far there have been 9,055 VFCs, 5,520 VFPCs and 640 unregistered groups formed in the state and they are involved in taking care of the management and protection of around 1,21,460 hectares, 6,51,545 hectares and 89,864 hectares of forest area in the state forest respectively (Department of Forest and Environment, Government of Odisha, 2011).

In spite of these natural endowments, Odisha is regarded as one of the most backward states in India. The Odisha's economy is characterized by low per capita income, low capital formation and inadequate exploitation of plentiful natural resources and poor development of socio-economic infrastructure. Moreover, poverty along with severe unemployment is also widespread in the state. As per the estimates of the Planning Commission, 47 percent of population is below poverty line in contrast to an all-India average of 26 percent. Unemployment is also a formidable problem. It has been estimated that the total backlog of unemployment at the beginning of 1999-2000 was of the order of 8.27 lakh. The magnitude of unemployment would be severe in future owing to growing population and lower employment opportunities being generated in the state. It is also observed that forests are yet to be fully utilized by the state over the last five decades to mitigate the magnitude of poverty and unemployment, due to a number of social, political, economic and climatic factors.

The study was carried out in Keonjhar district (tribal dominated district) of Odisha where community-based forest resource management institutions under the aegis of JFM have been established since 1995. The primary purpose of this micro-level study was to investigate the access of the forest dwelling population into the forest resource and the management in the context of emerging changes in the forest policies, and also their impact on the sustainable livelihood of forest dependent communities. Four tribal dominated villages in Anandapur and Ghasipura blocks in Keonjhar district of Odisha were selected on the basis of largest forest coverage area under CPRs, largest percentage of CPR area declining and their participatory development on Forest Protection Committees (FPCs) under JFM. The sample villages were finally selected on the basis of operation of JFM area and their participation of both poor and non-poor households for protecting the village forest land in consultation with the local DFOs and senior forest officials. The selected villages were Kantipal and Kolimati in Anandapur block and Madanpur and Birgovindpur in Ghasipura block.

The study is based on primary and secondary sources of data. Primary data on household level variables, their dependency on forest land for their livelihood and management of community forestry were collected in four villages through three different structured schedules, namely, village schedule, household schedule, schedule for local level institutions and NGOs pertaining to the year 2009. A separate schedule was prepared asking all the households seeking answers to a multiple objective type questions pertaining to their perception and understanding of forest Act, rules, policy, forest conservation, access to forest resources, participation in the protection of village forest and plantation of degraded forest land through JFM on different category of households. In the field investigation, 200 households were covered by using household schedule covering four important areas, namely, demographic, land holding pattern, dependency on forests for their livelihood and their participation in management and utilization of forests under JFM.

Therefore, we adopted a multi-stage sampling method to select poor and non-poor households of participant and non-participant households under JFM for protecting the village forest land. The poor households included landless labourers, agricultural workers, artisans, small farmers (≥ 1.00 ≤ 1.99 ha. of land) and marginal farmers (≤0.99 ha. of land). The non-poor households included servicemen and small entrepreneurs, very large farmers (> 9.99 ha), large (≥ 5.00 ≤ 9.99 ha.), upper middle (≥3.00 ≤ 4.99ha.) and lower middle (≥2.00 ≤ 2.99 ha.) farmers. Sample households were then selected from each village after giving proper weightage to each category.

Table 9.1 shows that the total number of households for intensive field survey was 200 households: 120 poor and 80 non-poor. Among the poor households, the proportion of scheduled tribes was the highest at 40 percent followed by other backward classes (24.2 percent), schedules castes (19.1 percent) and general castes (16.7 percent) in that order. Agriculture was the primary occupation of all the sample households in the study villages. All the sample households belonging to different classes and castes were dependent on

CPRs for their livelihood for collection of fuel wood, food, fodder, timber and non-timber forest product (NTFP) such as harida, bahada, mahula, kendu, sal leave, mango, jamu, jackfruit, sal seeds, medicinal and herbal plants for their domestic consumption and sale. They sell their products through middlemen who are mostly non-tribal. The land use pattern of the study villages was categorized as cultivated land, area not available for cultivation, village forest area, and cultivable waste and grazing land.

Table 9.1: Distribution of the Sample Households by Caste and Class

Name of the Village	Category of Household	No. of Sample Households by Caste				
		SC	ST	OBC	GC	All
Madanpur	Poor	4	6	9	7	26
	Non-poor	5	4	6	5	20
	All	9	10	15	12	46
Kolimati	Poor	5	15	6	4	30
	Non-poor	3	9	4	2	18
	All	8	24	10	6	48
Birgovin-pur	Poor	*6*	*11*	*8*	7	*32*
	Non-poor	7	9	4	2	22
	All	13	20	12	9	54
Kantipal	Poor	8	16	6	2	32
	Non-poor	4	6	6	4	20
	All	12	22	12	6	52
All Villages	Poor (percent)	23 (19.1)	48 (40.0)	29 (24.2)	20 (16.7)	120 (100.0)
	Non-poor (percent)	19 (23.7)	28 (35.0)	20 (25.0)	13 (16.3)	80 (100.0)
	All (percent)	42 (21.0)	76 (38.0)	49 (24.5)	33 (16.5)	200 (100.0)

Figures in parenthesis are percentages of total.
Source: Field Survey.

Apart from this classification, these four villages have provided access rights to the protection and management of state forests. Though caste structure is heterogeneous, comprising of various castes, such as, *Brahmins, Khandayat, Teli, Sudras* and *Tribals*, the tribals constitute the dominant group in all the study villages. Moreover, it has been found that a large proportion of the total population in these villages are subsistence farmers and forest dwellers. During the lean agricultural season, when there is no agricultural work, they also earned their livelihood as wage labourers in the construction of village roads under Mahatma Gandhi National Rural Employment Guarantee Scheme (MGNREGS), Pradhan Mantri Gram Sadak Yojana (PMGSY) and other poverty alleviation programmes. The villages were surrounded by forests from all sides. Besides collecting products from forests, the main occupation of villagers was encroachment on forest land for cultivation purpose. But the main occupation of STs in the sample villages were hunting, food gathering from forests for their personal use and sale of these products to outside traders and also encroachment on forest land for cultivation.

Under secondary data, information about sample JFM village and the history of their establishment, their land use pattern, demographic trend and forest resources were collected from the respective forest blocks. A lot of valuable secondary source information was collected from the Department of Forest and Environment, Government of Odisha, SC and ST Welfare Department, Principal Chief Conservation of Forest Office, Economic Survey, statistical abstracts, statistical handbooks, periodicals and journals etc.

People's Participation under JFM in Study Villages

Joint forest management (JFM) as a programme had its beginning in the district of Keonjhar in 1995 in eleven selected villages. Our four sample villages namely Kolimati, Kantipal, Madanpur and Birgovindpur were reported to have adopted JFM in 2000. Accordingly, around 177 hectares of land was taken up for the purpose of plantation and protection of existing forests under the social forestry programme as reported by the village leaders and *sarpanch* in these sample villages since the formation of JFM in 2000. Various groups were formed and responsibilities were distributed among them. One male and one female from each JFM household of the village were nominated as members of JFM. The JFM committees initially resolved to form protection group to watch and ward in order to prevent illegal feeling of trees. However, people of all JFM households in all sample villages were very enthusiastic to protect their forest than the non-JFM sample households. The village Birogovindpur had the highest JFM household members i.e., 63 percent (34 household members) followed by Kolimati almost 52 percent (26 household members), Madanpur 50 percent (23 household members) and Kantipal 42 percent (22 household members). Almost 55 percent (66 household members) of sample poor households were members of JFM whereas it was around 49 percent (39 household members) of non-poor household. Overall, it was 52 percent (105 household members) under JFM households as shown in Table 9.2.

During 2000-01, people of all these sample villages among JFM households were engaged in watch and ward of their forest on rotation basis. But, since 2004, JFM committees have engaged paid watchers with payment of ₹ 700 per month in Kolimati, ₹ 500 per month in Birgovindpur since 2003, ₹ 600 per month in Madanpur since 2004 and ₹ 800 per month in Kantipal since 2005 for protection of the forests due to conflict between JFM and non-JFM households.

The watchers carry out other activities as per the needs and decisions of the JFM committee. The village members are provided with requisite permission by the committee to collect NTFPs and wood as per their requirements. The timber for the construction of houses by the villagers is primarily examined and permitted by the village committee.

Table 9.2 reveals that around 31 percent household members (63 out of 200 sample households) in all villages actively participated in joint forest management (JFM). The active participation on JFM by the poor was nearly 34 percent (41 out of 120 sample households) than the non-poor households which was around 27 percent (22 out of 80 sample households). The active participation on JFM among four sample villages varied between 23 percent (in Kantipal village) to nearly 39 percent (in Birgovindapur village). There were village forest committees since 2000 in all sample villages consisting of 105 household members in pen and paper but work was being done by the forest department to involve the local people in the management of forest.

Table 9.2: Participation on Category of Sample Households on JFM (VFCs/VSSs/FPCs)

Name of the Village	Category of Households	No. of Households	JFM (VFC/VSS/ FPC) Households (No.)	Non-JFM Households (No.)
Madanpur	Poor	26	12	14
	Non-poor	20	11	9
	All	46	23	23
Kolimati	Poor	30	18	12
	Non-poor	18	8	10
	All	48	26	22
Birgovindpur	Poor	32	21	11
	Non-poor	22	13	9
	All	54	34	20
Kantipal	Poor	32	15	17
	Non-poor	20	7	13
	All	52	22	30
All Villages	Poor	120	66	54
	Non-poor	80	39	41
	All	200	105	95

Contd...

Name of the Village	Percentage of Participation of JFM Households in Total Households	Active Participation of Households in JFM (No.)	Percentage of Active Participation of JFM Households in Total Households
Madanpur	46.2	7	26.9
	55.0	5	25
	50.0	12	26
Kolimati	36.7	12	40
	44.4	6	33.3
	54.2	18	37.5
Birgovindpur	65.6	14	43.7
	59.1	7	31.8
	63.0	21	38.8
Kantipal	46.9	8	25
	35.0	4	20
	42.3	12	23
All Villages	55.0	41	34.1
	48.8	22	27.5
	52.5	63	31.5

Source: Field Survey.

There were various problems in all sample villages. First, Forest Protection Committees (FPCs) were set up in haste and superfluous action without adequate consultation with other local communities.

Second, there was a conflict among different caste and tribal groups, for instance Juang and Bhuiyan, SCs (Pana) and OBCs (Teli, Gopala), sometimes leading to violence for protection of village forest area.

Third, the forest dwellers were getting small timber and firewood from forest formally or informally. But they did not get any additional incentive in these items for their own use under the JFM scheme. A Government of Odisha resolution in 1993 on JFM offered 50 percent share in any major/final harvest and 100 percent of intermediate products to forest protection committee, called as Vana Sanrakhyan Samiti. Joint forest management seeks to involve and treat local communities as equal partners in the task of protection and management of forests. But the misbalanced power relationship between Forest department and local communities in all sample villages makes this a remote reality. Local communities find JFM unacceptable since this tends to erode decision-making at community level and also disregards the traditional knowledge system of the community. The restriction on sale of gathered firewood or small timber was unrealistic as many of the poor forest dwellers depend on sale of these forest produce for their subsistence. Under JFM, Forest Department plays an important role in decisions relating to forests.

Fourth, in absence of general body, the forest protection committee was not always representative of all different sections of forest users of the village. Fifth, the rights and tenures of the community over forest patch were not specified. Only certain concessions for fulfilling the requirements were spelt out—there was no mention of any share in the intermediate or final harvest in the sample villages.

Apart from protecting the forests from further degradation, their participative management, involving all the rural households, particularly the rural poor, promotes the social bond across families at the village level. This will help both poor as well as the non-poor. For example, in the past, the poor maintained the livestock of the rich on common grazing lands and in turn used to pay for their services in terms of cash, fodder, fuel wood and livestock. This was both a means to strengthen the social bond at the village as also an assured source of income to the poor. In our study villages, though the development agencies have tried and succeeded in protecting and regenerating the degraded forest land, they have failed in involving all sections of the rural society in such developmental programme.

It appears that the share of poor households in the biomass from the forests may further decline as the quantity and quality of biomass from it increases. This is because it is the non-poor who have an absolute control over the use and management of such resources. Even while taking up the degraded forests for development, it appears that all the households were never consulted or involved. No doubt the officials along with representatives of the rich might have persuaded one or two poor households to accept the scheme. In reality, however, there was no active involvement or participation. The poor as a result of their socio-political and economic submission to the non-poor hardly express their clear views. Keeping the poor in the background, a few representatives of the rich try to commercialize and gain from the forest land. In one village, the forest officials have tried to form the village committee to manage the forests, by involving all households. But in practice no committee is active. The leader of the village (elite) plays his own games as does the leader of the poor.

Further, it may be interesting to understand how actually the rural poor perceive the forests. In other words, to what extent will they protect the village forests by their participation in the use and management through JFM, if equal chance is given. What we have noticed through our own discussions with the poor households in the sample villages is that, even these households largely prefer the available village forest land to be distributed among them as private property resources (PPRs). The reasons for this reaction may be due to: (i) unequal distribution of PPRs (land and livestock) among the rural families, (ii) lack of forest-based PPRs among the poor, (iii) neglect of non-market forces in the rural economy, and (iv) lack of proper policy by the government about forest land, particularly, regularization of the encroached forests. Thus, in such a situation, promoting participation from all sections of the rural society in the use and management of forests under JFM seems to be a difficult task.

Involvement of NGOs and Panchayat Raj Institution

Odisha has a rich tradition of institutional pluralism. The role of NGOs can be classified into three categories. These are: (i) service providers, (ii) facilitators, and (iii) activists. A look at the activities of NGOs reveals that a majority of them are in the first and second categories. Most of the NGOs in the state indicate that they are engaged in a variety of activities including the forest sector and as such very few NGOs have mentioned forest related activities as their main role. However, the non-governmental sector has taken a keen interest in the forestry sector. There are of course some important NGOs such as the Regional Centre for Development Corporation (RCDC) and Vasundhara who mainly deal with forestry. These organizations have combined all the three types of role, including activism in policy formulation and policy changes in the state. There are many NGOs which are working in forest-related activities but whose names are not found in any directories. The Government of India (GoI) has recommended that NGOs be invited to help promote joint forest management. However, it has permitted only a limited role for them. The JFM letter from the GoI stated that the NGOs are "particularly well suited for motivating and organizing village communities for protection, afforestation and development of degraded forest land" (GoI, 1990).

There are some NGOs in the study villages, which provide services for development of forests and forest fringe people. For instance, there are some NGOs including Vikalpa, Vasundhara and Agragami, in Kanipal and Kolimati village of Anandapur block and Madanpur and Birgovindpur village of Ghasipura block, which are associated with development of forest-related activities. These NGOs are working in organizing the people especially tribals, whose livelihood is dependent on the development of forests through social forestry and forest-related activities. It has played an active role in all the three activities associated with NGOs. It covers around 76 hectares of land of all sample villages during reference time period as per the report of sarpanch in these study villages since the formation of JFM. Sometimes, they are service providers and play an anti-government role with a view to highlight the plight of the forest dwellers and/or the inadequacy of services provided by the government of the day. Agragami's role is an example of this type.

The panchayat raj institution at the village level in all the study villages is weak and has no capacity to deal with NTFP trade. In reality, its role has been marginal. In operational terms, now the traders who want to operate in these villages have to register in their respective panchayat and pay a fixed price to the village level committee. Overall the panchayats have been provided with the responsibility and authority of managing NTFP, but the lack of capacity both in terms of manpower and funds to exercise these powers is a hindrance and in many cases they are not aware of their powers also. As such, the recent changes in the policies of NTFPs are yet to improve the livelihood condition of the forest dwellers. As per the JFM deal, 100 percent of the intermediate produce and 50 percent of any major harvest is supposed to go the forest protection committees (FPCs)/Vana Samrakshyan Saimties (VSS). Thus, VSS should get 100 percent of NTFPs, but VSS members and NTFP gatherers get only wages for collection of some of these products in study villages. Thus, even on supposedly jointly managed forest land, the co-managers are treated as mere labourers, which are to gather NTFPs and hand over to state appointed agents at the state fixed prices. The state fixed prices are based on minimum wages principles and are not based on the value of the produce. Recently, there have been some changes in the NTFP policy, but still the state has retained control over the major revenue earning of NTFP items and has handed over only 68 'minor' MFPs to gram panchayats.

Even in the case of gram panchayats, the transfer is not complete in the study villages. For instance, according to the 2000 resolution, in fact the panchayat has been given only a rudimentary role. Although the policy says that panchayat are the owners of the NTFPs, in reality, they have been given a minor role with regard to the trade of NTFP simply to perform the registration of traders on payment of specified fee. Interlocking of credit and output of market, forces the gatherers to sell their produce to the money lenders at pre-determined prices. Further, pressing needs to generate cash and the limited surplus of forest products erodes their bargaining capacity and makes them more vulnerable to exploitation. Even the price realized by the selling of nationalized forest products such as *kendu* leaves is very low. Often the sellers do not receive the price on time. Another reason for low prices for the produce is the lack of value addition at the village level. For instance, the sale of cups and plates in the study villages made up of *sal/siali* leaves could be done through a low priced machine rather than the current practice of handmade, machine stitched products which could have fetched a better price for the sellers. There is hardly any effort by the forest department or NGOs in such value addition.

There are restrictions with respect to storage, transportation, marketing and processing of NTFPs in the study villages. They prefer generally to sell NTFPs to middlemen, traders and agents. It appears that the restrictions on permits, registration etc. are an essential part of forest laws and policies. The objectives of these are ostensibly to ensure sustainable management of NTFP resources and ecological and environmental sustainability (and not only to raise greater amount of royalty). In practice, these cause a variety of adverse effects on the livelihood options of indigenous communities. Further, VSS institutions, in the absence of legal authority, have failed to resolve many inter-personal conflicts prevalent in the groups. In such situations, VSS committee finds it difficult to take strong action against erring individuals or the state for non-compliance. It also becomes difficult to ensure equitable distribution of usufructs given the prevailing socio-economic inequalities in the rural communities.

It has been found that in the study villages, poorer members in the groups, whether in JFM or non-JFM, are unable to realize fully the benefits accruing from the forest protection. The participation of women is also weak. In some cases, group's dependence on their traditional occupation such as bamboo works, hunting and gathering of timber and non-timber forest produces, makes it difficult to get the benefits since the JFM executive committee prohibits utilization of bamboo and NTFPs for a certain time period. Such situation leads to exclusion of many poor from benefit sharing.

Income and Employment from Forests under JFM and Non-JFM Households

The total dependency of households on the forest land has been calculated by summing up the total income derived from fuel wood, food, fodder, and small timber and non-timber forest products (NTFPs).The average total income received by the households who are participating in the JFM activities is presented as Table 9.3. An examination of the data in the table indicates that poor household gets maximum benefits than non-poor household in terms of income from forests which are being managed by the forest protection committees under JFM. It can be seen from Table 9.3 that poor households derived on an average, gross income of ₹ 11,550 per household from forests and non-poor households derived ₹ 11,651 under the JFM. The average gross annual income of the poor households from the forests ranged between ₹ 8,546 and ₹ 12,621 in different study villages during the reference period. The source income from forests for the non-poor ranged between ₹ 9,651 and ₹ 13,432. In the study villages, apart from the benefits of the development, it is the non-poor who exploit the available forests to a greater extent.

Table 9.3: Average Gross Income Generated from Forests by JFM Households (₹ per annum)

Name of the Village	Category of Households	No. of JFM Households	AGI per Household from All Sources	AGI per Household from Forests	Forests Income as percent of AGI per Household
Madanpur	Poor	12	18456	8546	46.3
	Non-poor	11	22731	9651	42.5
	All	23	20501	9074	44.3
Kolimati	Poor	18	19452	12561	64.6
	Non-poor	8	21849	12697	58.1
	All	26	20190	12603	62.4
Birgovindpur	Poor	21	21753	11634	53.5
	Non-poor	13	26542	11742	44.2
	All	34	23584	11675	49.5
Kantipal	Poor	15	20672	12621	61.1
	Non-poor	7	25561	13432	52.5
	All	22	22228	12879	57.9
All Villages	Poor	66	20280	11550	57.0
	Non-poor	39	24328	11651	47.9
	All	105	21784	11587	53.2

AGI = Average Gross Income.
Source: Field Survey.

Though the poor households get much less average gross income per household from forests as compared to the non-poor household, it is relatively more important in their household budget in all the study villages. But the share (percent) of average gross income per household from forests to average gross income per household from all sources is higher among the poor as compared to the non-poor households in our study villages managed by FPCs under JFM. However, despite the non-poor getting greater absolute benefit, a greater proportion of the household income of the poor was derived from forests under JFM. This proportion varied from 46 percent of the gross income per household in Madanpur village to 64 percent in Kolimati village and for all the sample poor households it was 57 percent of their income from forests managed by FPCs under JFM.

Hence, on an average more than half of the income of the poor was derived from the forests, whereas it was 48 percent for the non-poor and 53 percent for the entire household in the reference period. Even in the case of the non-poor, the contribution of forests income as a proportion of gross income per household varied from 42 percent in Madanpur to 58 percent in Kolimati under JFM.

The average total income received by the households who are not participating in the JFM activities under non-JFM households is presented as Table 9.4.

In all the study villages, the poor households earned 42 percent and the non-poor got 37 percent in terms of income from forests under non-JFM, but overall, it was 39 percent of all non-JFM households during the reference period as shown in Table 9.4.

The non-poor earn about 30 percent in Madanpur village to 46 percent in Kolimati village of their income from forests under the non-JFM households across the study villages; the poor households earn about 35 percent in Madanpur to 52 percent in Kolimati of their total income from forests in all the study villages.

An examination of the data indicates that JFM households got maximum benefits than non-JFM household in terms of income from forests which are being managed by the forest protection committees under JFM due to effective participation and proper functioning.

Data in Table 9.5 establishes the fact that the poor households under JFM substantially gain from the employment opportunities generated due to effective and proper functioning of FPC in our study villages.

It is found that the poor households under JFM gained 168 days of employment in the forest-related activities per year in all the study villages as compared to non-poor households who were engaged for 109 days, but overall under the JFM households, it was 146 days per year.

Table 9.4: Average Gross Income Generated from Forests under Non-JFM Households (₹ per annum)

Name of the Village	Category of Households	No. of Non-JFM Households	AGI per Household from all Sources	AGI per Household from Forests	Forests Income as percent of AGI per Household
Madanpur	Poor	14	16246	5746	35.4
	Non-poor	9	22731	6351	27.9
	All	23	18784	5983	31.9
Kolimati	Poor	12	16452	8511	51.7
	Non-poor	10	20849	9607	46.1
	All	22	18451	9009	48.8
Birgovindpur	Poor	11	18753	8064	43
	Non-poor	9	22542	9342	41.4
	All	20	20458	8639	42.2
Kantipal	Poor	17	18632	7221	38.8
	Non-poor	13	21761	7432	34.2
	All	30	19988	7312	36.6
All Villages	Poor	54	17554	7297	41.6
	Non-poor	41	21923	8144	37.2
	All	95	19439	7663	39.4

AGI = Average Gross Income.
Source: Field Survey.

In fact, JFM is very effective and successful in these villages due to more participation of poor households than non-poor and the implementation of micro plan for plantation and proper commercialization of NTFPs which were instrumental in creating huge employment opportunities throughout the year for all the participants of 105 households irrespective of their standard of living.

Furthermore, it is found that poor households also got substantial man-days of employment and on an average more than four people were engaged in forests per year from the forest-related activities as compared to three people of non-poor households under the JFM.

Table 9.5: Average Employment, Time Spent and Distance Covered for Forest Produce under JFM Households

Name of the Village	Category of Households	No. of JFM Households	Annual Average Day Employed per Collection of Forest Produce (No. of Days)	Annual Average People Employed for Forest Produce
Madanpur	Poor	12	128	5
	Non-poor	11	86	6
	All	23	108	5
Kolimati	Poor	18	198	6
	Non-poor	8	134	5
	All	26	178	6
Birgovindpur	Poor	21	151	5
	Non-poor	13	98	4
	All	34	131	5
Kantipal	Poor	15	186	5
	Non-poor	7	136	4
	All	22	170	5
All Villages	Poor	66	168	6
	Non-poor	39	109	5
	All	105	146	6

Contd...

Name of the Village	Average Time Spent per Collection of Forest Produce (Hours)	Average Distance Covered per Collection Forest-related Activities	Accessibility (Percentage of People who felt Forest Produce is Open)
Madanpur	4.54	3.03	33.3
	6.04	3.12	27.3
	5.26	3.07	30.4
Kolimati	6.42	3	33.3
	5.31	3	37.5
	6.08	3	34.6
Birgovindpur	5.27	2.48	57.1
	5.01	3.52	46.2
	5.17	2.88	52.9
Kantipal	5.67	2.88	40
	6.42	3.37	57.1
	5.91	3.04	45.5
All Villages	5.54	2.81	42.4
	5.62	3.27	41
	5.57	2.98	41.9

Source: Field Survey.

While non-JFM poor households gained 121 days of employment of forest-related activities as compared to 85 days of non-poor households engaged in all the sample villages, but overall, it was 106 days per year (Table 9.6). Therefore, it can be concluded that an effective FPC plays a pivotal role in generating ample employment opportunities and income compared to the non-participant households under JFM in our study area.

Tables 9.5 and 9.6 also show that the distance between the place of dwelling (habitation) and source of fuel wood collection (forest) was around 3 km., but to collect fuel wood, the people had to go deep into the forest due to degradation of forests and congestion of fuel wood collectors. It was observed in the study villages that women and children aged between 10 and 15 years belonging to the poor households cover over 3 to 4 kms. in JFM household and 2 to 3 kms. in non-JFM households of CPRs (including road sides) for dead and fallen wood, twigs, thorny bushes, dry leaves, roots etc. If wages on labour days spent on such type of fuel wood collection are calculated, even a child has to be paid more than the average wage rate in many other villages. This resulted in an increase in the time spent on fuel wood collection. The average time spent per collection of fuel wood varied between a minimum of four hours and a maximum of seven hours in case of poor households and five to seven hours of non-poor households under JFM and non-JFM households.

It is generally understood that CPRs like a forest are completely accessible to the people. But in reality people do not have total access to all types of forests. Forest authorities (the forest department) regulate accessibility to the forest area specially when these are under reserve forest or protected area category. Nearly 42 percent of the poor, 41 percent of non-poor and 42 percent of all households in the study villages felt that the forest was open for fuel wood collection without any restriction under the JFM household.

Table 9.6: Average Employment, Time Spent and Distance Covered for Forest Produce under Non-JFM households

Name of the Village	Category of Households	No. of Non-JFM Households	Annual Average Day Employed per Collection of Forest Produce (No. of Days)	Annual Average People Employed for Forest Produce
Madanpur	Poor	14	102	3
	Non-poor	9	67	4
	All	23	88	3
Kolimati	Poor	12	147	2
	Non-poor	10	107	3
	All	22	129	2
Birgovindpur	Poor	11	111	4
	Non-poor	9	78	3
	All	20	96	4
Kantipal	Poor	17	126	4
	Non-poor	13	86	2
	All	30	109	3
All Villages	Poor	54	121	3
	Non-poor	41	85	3
	All	95	106	3

Contd...

Name of the Village	Average Time Spent per Collection of Forest Produce (Hours)	Average Distance Covered per Collection of Forest-related Activities	Accessibility (Percentage of People who felt Forest Produce is Open)
Madanpur	5.24	2.56	57.1
	4.45	3.12	66.7
	4.93	2.78	60.9
Kolimati	6.32	2.96	66.7
	5.21	3.13	50
	5.82	3.04	77.3
Birgovindpur	5.17	2.48	63.6
	4.81	3.52	66.7
	5.01	2.95	65
Kantipal	6.17	2.88	35.3
	5.42	3.37	23.1
	5.85	3.09	30
All Villages	5.76	2.73	74.1
	5.02	3.29	53.7
	5.44	2.97	65.3

Source: Field Survey.

However, in case of non-JFM households it was opposite. Almost 74 percent of poor, 53 percent of non-poor and 65 percent of all households in the study village felt that forest produce had open access (Table 9.6).

If the present forests use structure continues unaltered, then the future for forest land in the study villages appears bleak. Due to the degradation of forest land, many households are already facing shortage of fuel wood and fodder. Many households have therefore started shifting towards other fuels such as dung cake—which constitutes wastage of precious potential manure—and inferior fuels like crop residue for cooking. The degradation of forest land has increased the time required for fuel wood collection and has resulted in the neglect and overexploitation of forests, which has further accelerated the degradation of forests. Thus, there has been a vicious circle of degradation and overexploitation of forest land. If this vicious circle is not broken, then the 'tragedy of common property resources' is certain to occur.

Conclusions and Policy Implication

In this study, we examined the relationship between poor and non-poor households with the income and employment opportunities from forests through JFM committee. It is found that the poor households through participation of FPCs derive larger benefits from the forest produce in contrast to the non-poor households under JFM and non-JFM. Further, the larger number of employment opportunities generated from the forests on FPCs goes to participation of poor households. The income from forests accounted for, on an average, more than half of the total income of the poor households and almost 48 percent of the total income of the non-poor households under JFM. Around 42 percent of the surveyed JFM households reported that the forest was open for fuel wood collection in contrast to 65 percent of non-JFM households. About 52 percent households participated in JFM committees whereas only 31 percent of sample households actively participated in the management of CPRs such as forest through joint forest management (JFM). Effective participation of local population, NGOs, panchayat raj institutions and equitable distribution of benefits did not happen in these villages, mainly due to institutional weaknesses.

JFM in the state as an institution is weak, which reflects the weakness of Odisha Forest Department as well as the FPCs. The JFM committee has been formed on the basis an administrative order of MoEF. There has been a lack of proper participatory process, either at the outset or post-formation. Local people's participation in the preparation of the 'micro plan' is generally marginal, as the forester exerts a major control over this. In the VSS executive committee and general body meetings, important decisions are taken by elites, including the forester (who is the secretary) in the study villages. Self-initiated groups were found to be to be more participatory than the VSS, although a few women are involved in JFM.

The important policy implication of this exercise is that both the state and the Central government should adopt strict JFM policy for implementation at the grass root level and also encourage the stakeholders to form community-based management institutions like FPCs under JFM policy for proper and effective utilisation of forests by adopting participatory approach in the rural areas. In protection, regeneration and developmental aspects of common property resources, more power should be entrusted to NGOs and the panchayati raj institutions with active participation of the local community to ensure equitable distribution of benefits. The government should integrate the JFM policy with ongoing poverty alleviation programmes in the forested area by providing both financial and logistical support for the effective management of the forest resources to accomplish the sustainable development goals in the forthcoming years.

Further, it should vigorously implement the JFM policy in tribal and poverty ridden forest areas with a view to generate additional income and employment base for the rural economy. JFM should be encouraged in the tribal areas of India to empower them more and more. FPCs should be formed for participation in the management of CPRs, such as forests, whereby both physical as well as socio-economic environment will improve significantly. Formation of self-help groups (SHGs) should be encouraged to meet the credit needs of the local people. Adequate storage facility for primary collectors of forest products should be provided with assistance from financial institutions. The rural households that derive benefits from forests should be convinced about the benefits of regeneration of forest land through plantation and sustainable utilization which will inspire the people to protect and regenerate them.

References

Adhikari, B. (2002), Property Rights and Natural Resource: Socio-Economic Heterogeneity and Distributional Implications of Common Property Resources and Management, EEE Working Papers Series, No. 3.

Anderson, K.E. (1995), Institutional Flows and Collective Forest Management, *Ambio,* Vol. 24, No. 6, pp. 349-353.

Ballabh, V. and Singh, K. (1988), Managing Forests Through People's Institutions: A Case Study of Van Panchayats in Uttar Pradesh Hills, *Indian Journal of Agricultural Economics,* Vol. 43, No. 3, pp. 296-305.

Behera, B. (2006), Determinants of Sustainable Management of Natural Resources: The Case of Joint Forest Management in India, Cuvillier Verlag, Gottingen.

Chopra, K., Kadekodi, G.K. and Murty, M.N. (1990), People Participation and Common Property Resources, *Economic and Political Weekly*, Vol. 24, No. 51, pp. A189-A195.

Government of India (GoI), (1990), Involvement of Village Communities and VAS in Regeneration of Degraded Forests: Circular on Joint Forest Management', Ministry of Environment and Forest, New Delhi.

Government of India (GoI), (2009), India State of Forest Report 2009, Forest Survey of India, Ministry of Environment and Forest, Dehradun.

Government of Odisha (GoO), (2011), Economic Survey 2011-12 and various other issues, Directorate of Economics and Statistics, Bhubaneswar, Odisha.

Government of Odisha (GoO), (2011), Annual Activities Report, 2010-11, Department of Forest and Environment, Bhubaneswar, Odisha.

Hardin, G. (1968), The Tragedy of Commons, *Science,* Vol. 162, pp. 1243-1248.

Hill, I. and D. Shields (1998), Incentives for Joint Forest Management in India: Analytical Methods and Case Studies, World Bank Techincal Paper No. 394, The World Bank, Washington D.C.

Jodha, N.S. (1986), Common Property Resources and Rural Poor in Dry Regions of India, *Economic and Political Weekly*, Vol. 21, No. 27, pp. 1169-1181.

Kumar, S. (2002), Does Participation in Common Pool Resource Management Help the Poor? A Social Cost-Benefit Analysis of Joint Forest Management in Jharkhand, India, *World Development*, Vol. 30, No. 5, pp. 763-782.

Rath, B. and Sahu, N.C. (2004), Revitalisation/Renovation of Common Property Resources (CPRs) Potentials as an Alternative Means to Improve the Economy of Odisha, in R.K. Panda (ed.) *Reviving Odisha Economy: Opportunities and Areas of Action,* APH Publishing Co., New Delhi.

Wade, R. (1987), The Management of Common Property Resources: Collective Action as an Alternative to Privatisation or State Regulation, *Cambridge Journal of Economics,* Vol. 11, pp. 95-106.

10

Management of Non-timber Forest Produce

K.A. Mohammed Noushad

Introduction

Kerala state, situated in the south western part of India at 8°18' north latitude and 74 °52' and 77 °22' east longitude covers an area of 38,863 sq. km. Of this, about 11309.4754 sq. km. are either natural forests or forest plantations. Physiographically, the State is divisible into four zones, namely the costal belt (<8 m above msl), the midlands (8-75m above msl), hilly uplands and the highlands (>75 m above msl) (Table 10.1).

Table 10.1: Details of Area under Different Forest Types in Kerala

Type	Area (sq. km.)	Percent
Tropical wet evergreen and semi-evergreen	3877.4413	34.28
Tropical moist deciduous	3615.9840	31.97
Tropical dry deciduous	391.3636	3.46
Montane sub-tropical temperate shoalas	386.4210	3.42
Plantations	1492.0287	13.19
Grass lands	501.0865	4.43
Others	1045.1503	9.24
Total	11309.4754	

The major habitat of non-wood forest produce (NWFP) plants of the State is the natural forests, occurring mainly in the hilly uplands and the highlands. This forest zone also includes forest plantations which, to some extent, form the natural abode of several NWFP species, less characteristic and ecologically more plastic. Midlands, which are essentially agricultural zone, also have sizeable NWFP species in the remnants of natural vegetation that flourish in sacred groves, wastelands and homesteads, where a few of them are also grown for their products. In the coastal belt of the State, the once luxuriant mangrove formation was rich in NWFP, for example medicinal plants. However, due to intensive agriculture, urbanisation or other developmental activities, coastal belt has now been impoverished to the maximum with regard to native flora and the NWFP plants which they contain.

Forest resources include both timber and non-timber produces. While timber products are available from natural forests, forest plantations and also from non-forest areas, non-timber forest produces are quite diverse and include plants, yielding items like medicine, food, fodder, gum, resin, spices, condiments, beverages, fibres, dyes and tans, ivory, honey, wax and few such items of animal origin. The products are either directly used by the tribal and rural people in their daily consumption or by the urban population. It is well understood that non-timber forest produces are of very high economic potential. And perhaps, this is the only commodity which can be readily sold in the world market without much global competition, as each country has a produce characteristic of its own and not produced or marketed by other countries (Table 10.2).

Management System of Non-Timber Forest Produces (NTFPs)

In Kerala, NTFPs are collected free of cost by Girijan co-operative societies and marketed by Kerala State Federation of SC and ST Development Co-operatives Ltd.

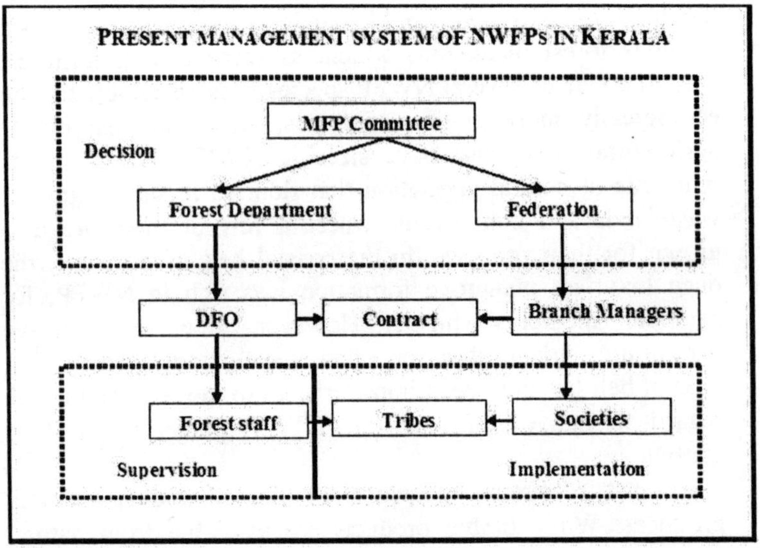

Table 10.2: Category-wise Production of NTFPs during 2009-2010

Name	Quantity (in kg.)
Ayurvedic herbs	64963.80
Spices	758.80
Fibre	13345.40
Grass other than fodder	73783.00
Incensive plants	21416.60
Vegetable oilseeds	3065.50
Honey	79268.90
Bee's wax	746.50
Parts of medicinal trees	12509.50

Issues and Concerns

Issues:

- Shrinking resource base and escalating demand.
- Destructive and exploitative practices.

Concerns:

- Sufficiency of resource.
- Sustenance and equity (spectrum of paternalism with spectrum of equity).

Imperatives of Conservation

- **Excessive and Destructive Extraction:** High rate of extraction of NTFPs carried out by the gatherers results in poor diversity, sparse distribution and depletion of biodiversity. Lured by high prices, the gatherers undertake intensive harvesting of premium items which results in changes in the species composition. This has detrimental effect on biodiversity of the landscape and depletion of resource.
- **Monetary Considerations:** In the context of commercial extraction, the prime consideration of the gatherers is to earn maximum income in the shortest time possible. They will resort to any method of collection, whether sustainable or not.
- **Absence of Hedging:** The collection charge has increased over time, but the real income of the tribal people from collection has not increased. The gatherers are getting low collection charge compared to final consumer price. As a result, their real income has not increased over time. In order to maintain their standard of living, intensive extraction of NTFPs is often resorted to, which affects biodiversity and sustainable use.
- **Proficiency of Intermediaries:** Although the Federation and societies are established to eliminate intermediaries, the latter still play a key role in the production and marketing chains and take maximum profit. Thus, the institutions are unable to protect the interests of the gatherers and consumers.
- **Non-versatile Management Approach:** Since societies and tribal people have no voice in the management of NTFPs, they do not show much interest in protecting and

conserving these resources. Given the shortcomings of present management system, though participatory management at local level would have been the best management system for the development of NTFPs, it has never been considered.

- **'Nil' Sense of Belonging:** Unless local people feel that they are a part of the system they will not show much interest to conserve the biodiversity. This calls for adoption of a better and alternative system of management of NTFPs giving more power to groups at the grass root level.
- **Institutional Constraints:** The Federation, the apex body of co-operative societies, gathers only premium products and thus, is not able to supply other items required by the user groups. This results in the decline of knowledge base of the tribal communities regarding NTFPs and increase of illegal collection by the non-tribals. The Federation has no professional managers. Marketing is its weakest link. NTFP trade is profitable, but the Federation is running in losses. Due to financial stringency, it is not in a position to carry out the programmes for the development of NTFPs.
- **Lack of Long-term Vision and Innovation:** The institutions such as the Federation and societies are established mainly to formulate and implement extraction strategies, streamline the management of NTFPs and uplift the socio-economic conditions of the tribal people. In the context of increased demand for certain products and consequent changes in prices, these institutions are forced to collect products having very high demand only. In a quarter of century of its existence, no effort has been made by the Federation either at value addition or marketing of any branded or niche product, the authenticity of which would have evoked tremendous response.
- **Absence of Enrichment Activities:** No attempt is made by the agencies relating to collection of NTFPs to prevent depletion by undertaking enrichment planting of any

species. For sustainable resource use, one needs to consider the regeneration rate of resources also (A study by Kerala Forest Research Institute, Peechi shows that in the case of vegetatively propagating species, the regeneration index is 100 percent or above even when the harvest is as high as 95 percent. On the other hand, in the case of plants regenerated through seeds, 35-50 percent is the sustainable limit).

- **Step Motherly Treatment:** Little or nil investment has been made to enhance the conservation, cultivation, trade and better understanding and improved use of such plants. While other cash crops have received research support worth millions of rupees, production of these exceptionally promising generators of income and well-being are left to languish and are therefore decreasing and many are in danger of disappearing.
- **Cross-sectoral Policy Impacts:** Kerala is targeting 2 lakh medical tourists by 2020 and the Government aims to make the State, one among the top five global players in medical tourism as part of its Vision 2020. Medical tourist arrival in Kerala has been increasing at an annual rate of 25-30 percent. In 90 percent of the cases the preferred system of treatment is Ayurveda. In the coming years, there is going to be an exponential growth in this segment. More the number of tourists, larger would be the mushrooming of treatment centres and consequent demand of herbal sources. Any decline in quality would entail reduced tourist arrival, resulting in huge dent in the tourist revenue which is going to be the mainstay industry of Kerala in the coming decades.

Remedies

While in-situ conservation forms the best and cost effective method for protecting biological and genetic diversity, this can adequately be complemented by ex-situ methods through cultivation. In the years to come, yield from the wild will not measure up to the escalating demand. In principle, many of the supply problems can be overcome by cultivating the medicinal plants. Supplies from the wild are at the mercy of the weather, pests, and other uncontrollable variables. But what looks like a problem, actually provides numerous opportunities, as farming these species would help even out the supply, regularize the trade, provide certifiable products of uniform quality, and make available to rural areas new sources of income. Through the process of cultivation, various plants can be increased on a controllable and sustainable basis, the quality can be better assured and species identification be made more secure. In addition, there are possibilities for improving the crop genetically based on the level and mix of ingredients that have medicinal effects. Yields can also be manipulated.

While natural ecosystems such as forests, wetlands and grasslands can be protected by legislations, many other medicinal plant habitats such as marginal, remote, wastelands, roadsides, or even gardens and hedges cannot be. An education program developed in collaboration with local collectors, dispensaries, and beneficiaries should be a priority.

The Lingering Dilemma

Even the most progressive farmers are reluctant to take up farming of medicinal plants due to lack of assured market and fair returns. They apprehend that in a glut market, fair price would be the first casualty, often citing the bad experience with cocoa and vanilla recently. Hurdle with industries is that long-term arrangement with farmers having limited holdings and production capabilities is unviable due to uncertainties and constraints of assured supply (deficiency/default in supply, breaches, derailed contracts, litigations etc.). Initiative by industries and guaranteed buy back arrangements will evolve and rally into collective or co-operative farming by 'the reluctant by experience' farming community. Tree crops with long gestation period and uncertain prospects of the yield, considering the time lag between investment and returns, is a hard nut to sell to farmers of Kerala, whether marginal or big. In a highly populous and land scarce state, acquiring large tract of land by private entrepreneurs is next to impossible and not cost efficient considering the prohibitive cost of land.

The Looming Gloom

The NTFP scenario in Kerala is unique, complex and intriguing—all at once. There is mounting demand for natural health care products from abroad and cash-rich corporate world; yet the farmers are reluctant to take up farming of medicinal plants despite conducive natural conditions; nursing wounds of the past and gazing at the unsure price movements and unpredictable market behaviour. In the prospective event/scenario of scarcity, spurious products would invade the market, denting the quality of services and in turn adversely impacting the current rating as the most favoured global medical tourism destination.

What Should be the Model for Future?

Kerala has 4,85,660 ha. under rubber cultivation, which is 83.15 percent of the gross area under this crop in India. The total number of trees per ha. is 420-500. The website of Rubber Board reads, "some shade tolerant medicinal plants like *Strobilanthus haemianus, Adathoda vasica* and *Plumbago rosea* are found to perform well as intercrops in rubber plantation. But the marketability should be ascertained before going for large scale cultivation". Intercrops should be planted at least 1.5 m away from the plant base. Intercrops should be separately nursed and adequately manured". The farmer should be able to produce medicinal plants at no extra cost or very marginal investment concurrent with other cash/main crops (yield from every yard), such that the returns are incidental and complement the returns from the preferred crop.

We have dispersed and unbridged islands of traditional knowledge and scientific expertise of modern times. There has to be a convergence of know how and do how. Silvicultural engineering of medicinal plants and cash crops and frontier technological innovations like precision farming hold the key for the future. Focused attention and concerted efforts of researchers and scientific community in this direction is the need of the hour.

References

Muraleedharan, P.K., U.M. Chandrashekara, K.K.Seethalakshmi and N. Sasidharan (1999), Biodiversity in Tropical Moist Forests: A Study of Sustainable Use of Non-Wood Forest Products in the Western Ghats; Kerala: Monitoring and Evaluation of Ecological and Socio-economic Variables, KFRI Research Report No. 162, Kerala Forest Research Institute, Peechi.

Nair, K.K.N. (2000), Manual of Non-Wood Forest Produce Plants of Kerala, KFRI Research Report No. 185, Kerala Forest Research Institute, Peechi.

Kerala Forest Department (2010), *Forest Statistics,* Thiruvananthapuram.

11

Managing Surface Water Resources

Ashok Kumar Maurya

Introduction

Fresh water is a unitary resource on planet and salvation of the human life and development. Long-term development of fresh water resources requires holistic management and recognition of the inter-connectedness of the elements related to freshwater and its quality. Water plays a complex multi-functional role for every human, plant and species on Earth. It is the most fundamental substance making life possible on our planet. In any conceivable scale, from global circulation system down to the individual cell, water is always present. A large number of resources have another substitute, but water, while fulfilling a number of purposes, has no substitute. Two-thirds of the planet is covered by the water and near about 97 percent of water is stored in the oceans in a saline form. Of the remaining 3 percent fresh water, 75 percent is stored as ice in Polar regions and is generally unavailable. Thus, only 1 percent of all water is free flowing fresh water and 98.8 percent of this lies at a considerable depth in the sub-surface. Only 1.2 percent of the available fresh water at a given time is in the form of surface water, unevenly distributed in lakes, rivers, clouds, groundwater and biological organisms (Dutta, 2005).

Gujarat is divided into four regions, Saurashtra, Kutch, South Gujarat and North Gujarat. The geographical location of the North Gujarat is 23^0 to 24^0.07' N Latitude and 71^0 to 73^0.07' E Longitude. North Gujarat has four districts, Mehsana, Patan, Sabarkantha and Banaskantha. A major part of the North Gujarat is suffering from groundwater degradation in form of contamination. The main reason of the water contamination is due to declining groundwater and fluoride being a main ingredient in bottomless groundwater. The Southern part of Gujarat region is endowed with some permanent rivers and North Gujarat region has better groundwater potential. This region is well-off in agriculture but it is mainly dependent on groundwater, both for irrigation and drinking water requirements. The irrigation infrastructure as well as the subsidy pattern of electricity has not taken care of sustained use of the water resources. The blueprint of exploitation so far has been highly uneven and unfriendly to the groundwater regimes.

Agricultural production in North Gujarat has rapidly increased over the last couple of decades, but this increment of agricultural production has been inflicted at the cost of unsustainable use of natural resources like land and groundwater. A large proportion of rural population of Gujarat depends on groundwater resources and agriculture is the largest consumer (75-80 percent) of water resources in Gujarat (Khan, 2008). Gujarat government planned a big scheme for drinking water named as Sardar Sarovar Master Plan in 1995 specially for North Gujarat. Basically, this plan is based on Narmada River and Sardar Sarovar Dam. This scheme has covered 14 districts of Ahmedabad, Amreli, Banaskantha, Sabarkantha, Mehsana, Bhavnagar, Jamnagar, Junagadh, Porbandar, Rajkot, Kachchh, Gandhinagar, Patan and Panchmahal. Other schemes like Sujalam Suphalam Yojana and Regional Water schemes are also functioning in North Gujarat for providing safe drinking water.

Drinking Water: A National Context

According to Rajiv Gandhi National Drinking Water Mission, some basic principles have ruled the drinking water supply.

Basic Principle:

1. Water is a public good and every person has the right to demand drinking water.

2. It is the lifeline activity of the government to ensure that this basic need of the people is met.
3. To increase economic productivity and improve public health, there is an urgent need to immediately enhance access to safe and adequate drinking water and government should give highest priority to meeting this basic need for the most vulnerable and deprived sections of the society.
4. The ethic of 'fulfillment of drinking water needs to all' should not be commercialized and denied to those who cannot afford to pay for such service.
5. Drinking water supply cannot be left to the market forces alone. The importance of providing livelihood supply to all and its vital linkage with the health of the people must be recognized.
6. As such, the emphasis should be more on public-public partnership (such as between gram panchayat and PHED for in-village distribution of drinking water) rather than commercialization of drinking water supply by private agencies.
7. User charges of the water supply system should have an in-built component of cross-subsidy to ensure that the economically backward groups are not deprived of this basic minimum need (RGNDWM, 2010).

Problem of Drinking Water in North Gujarat

The availability of the groundwater is not satisfactory because for the past some years, the quantity and quality of groundwater have been diminishing. The groundwater balance approach is negative and the rate of groundwater over-exploitation is much more, compared to groundwater recharge in Gujarat. The two main reasons for negative groundwater balance are: (i) the over-consumption of the groundwater, and (ii) lack of surface water resources like rivers, ponds etc. (Table 11.1). Presently, there is predominant use of groundwater for irrigation purpose. Other users of groundwater are industry and the domestic sectors.

Table 11.1: Region-wise Availability of Groundwater

Area	Million Cubic Meter
North Gujarat	3300
South Gujarat and Central Gujarat	3950
Saurashtra area	4300
Kutch	450

Source: Narmada, Water Resources, Water Supply and Kalpsar Department, Gujarat (2010).

Industrial user and rural irrigation tend to tap groundwater directly by own tubewells, borewells and dugwells. But urban demand for drinking and other civic uses is mainly met by municipal bodies which tap both groundwater and surface water sources like lakes, rivers and canals. This urban demand though very small in comparison to agricultural demand, is rising at a high rate (Dhawan, 1995).

Gujarat has a diverse geological, hydrological, climatic and soil conditions, all of which has implications on the status of surface and groundwater resources in the state. Gujarat's drinking water problems are not limited to availability of water, but also extend to quality of drinking water used by rural communities. Gujarat is a water stressed state, with its per capita availability of fresh water at 1,137 cubic meter compared to less than 1,700 cubic meter per year at satisfactory level (Hirway, 2005). In the past two decades, the state has lost about 27 percent of its ground water resources, the loss being 50 percent in North Gujarat (Hirway, 2005). Water borne diseases resulting from contaminated drinking water and poor sanitation have been rampant in the state since the last decade. About 78 percent of the rural water supply in Gujarat is dependent on groundwater, of which only 2 percent is utilized for drinking purposes (WASMO, 2010).

In a large area of the state, over drafting of groundwater mainly for agriculture and subsequent depletion of aquifers has had a great impact on the water availability during the recent past. Water problem is becoming a central topic of debate in Gujarat. With the possible exception of perennial rivers in south Gujarat, surface sources within the state are extensively developed. The groundwater level in North Gujarat has been rapidly depleting by 3-5 meters every year due to over-exploitation of groundwater for domestic, agriculture and industrial uses. The state has 5.96 percent of nation's geographical area and 5 percent of the population but has only 2.63 percent of country's water resource. It has been estimated that about half the villages in the state face serious shortage of potable drinking water in the summers.

During the pre-Independence period, there was no serious problem of drinking water reported in the state, except for a few references to shortages of drinking water in some situations. This was largely due to the fact that groundwater situation was fairly good in most parts of the state without water contamination and it was available even during droughts. The problem of drinking water acquired significant dimensions gradually with the increased use of groundwater in irrigation on the one hand and the declining traditional water systems of managing local water supply on the other hand. An additional factor that has contributed to the problem is the decline of the traditional local systems of water supply. Traditional water supply was managed through local systems in most of the villages in the North Gujarat. These local systems seem to have declined because of two main reasons, namely: (i) over drafting of groundwater depleted local water resources very badly leaving no adequate water supply, in terms of quality and quantity, for local people (Bhatia, 1992), and (ii) local water supply system was managed by government organizations, GWSSB and GWIL and they are responsible organization for providing safe drinking water.

Regional disparity is extremely high for freshwater in this region. The south and central zones, which have major rivers like Narmada, Mahi, Tapi, Ambica, Poorna, etc., and forested areas, have 1,932 ppm. per capita per annum of fresh water. This is equivalent to 70 percent of the state freshwater availability. In Kutch, it is 875 ppm. per capita per annum and in Saurashtra, it is 624 per capita per annum, whereas North Gujarat has lowest freshwater availability with 427 ppm per capita per annum. The Gujarat Water and Sewage Board (GWSSB) has declared more than 75 percent villages in the state as 'no sources village' which means villages with no dependable or sustainable sources of water (Table 11.2).

Table 11.2: Households Access to Drinking Water (Taps, Handpumps and Tubewells) in Gujarat

(in percentage)

Year	Urban	Rural
1981	86.8	36.2
1991	87.2	60.0
2001	95.2	76.9

Source: Economic Survey, 2010-11; Office of the Registrar General, Ministry of Home Affairs.

The water quality dilemma in terms of excessive fluoride content as well as salinity was observed in significantly high number of habitations with Dangs being the only district without any quality affected sources. Moreover, new areas were also budding as being quality affected. The gap between demand and supply of domestic water is negative and water supply for rural areas is not sufficient for domestic exercise. The rural population constitutes about 65 percent of the total population and they consume about 42 percent of the total domestic water supply in Gujarat.

Saurashtra has more than 25 percent of the total rural population, but the population consumes only about 16 percent of the total water supply. Kachchh has 3.4 percent of the total rural population, but the population consumes only 2.4 percent of the total water supply. The corresponding percentages are 50.70 percent and 56.93 percent for South Gujarat and 20.7 percent and 24.58 percent for North Gujarat respectively. Saurashtra and Kachchh receive much less than 40 liters per capita per day of water supply, which is also much less than the state average of 42 liters per capita per day (Hirway, 2005).

Sources of Surface Drinking Water in North Gujarat

In North Gujarat, there are two types of water resources, Narmada river resources water and Regional water schemes. SSCB and SSY schemes are running on the Narmada river and Regional Water Supply Schemes and Individual Piped Water Supply Projects are working on groundwater resources. Narmada water is supplied by the Narmada main canal and dams that are a mass of the surface water and pumped with the help of bulk pipe line to each village that are under the SSCB and SSY schemes. Under the Regional Water Supply Schemes, water resources located in one place are used by a large number of villages, where the water is transported through pipelines. In some cases, water is transported to distances of more than 200 km. At present, there are about 392 regional schemes which cover about 4,432 villages in the state (Jal Disha, 2010). Individual Piped Water Supply Projects is a village level project where each village has its own water supply facilities and provides drinking water in the villages.

Surface Water Management in Gujarat

Sardar Sarovar Narmada Nigam Ltd. (SSNNL) was set up by the State Government to implement the Sardar Sarovar (Narmada) Project in the year 1988. The Sardar Sarovar Dam is a dam on the Narmada River near Navagam, Gujarat. It is the largest dam and part of the Narmada Valley Project. The Sardar Sarovar Project is a multi-purpose project, which envisages construction of concrete gravity dam across the river Narmada in Narmada district. It envisages a 458 km. long main canal with a discharge capacity of 4,000 cusecs at starting point and 2,500 cusecs at Gujarat-Rajasthan border with a network of 74,626 km. for water distribution system for irrigation purposes. Amongst the 30 large dams planned for the Narmada, the Sardar Sarovar dam is the largest.

The Sardar Sarovar Dam was partially completed in August 2008. The dam is irrigating 17,920 sq. km. of land and provides drinking water facility to over 12 districts, 62 talukas and 3,393 villages in Gujarat. The project will provide annual irrigation benefits in an area of about 18.45 lakh hectares spread over 73 talukas of 15 districts in the State. It is also envisaged to provide water for domestic and industrial uses in about 9,633 villages and 131 townships. About three-fourth of the command area under this project is drought prone as defined by the Irrigation Commission (Socio-Economic Review, 2010-11).

The Narmada water for drinking and sanitation is visualized for augmenting the supply significantly from a bare minimum of 25 to 40 liters per capita per day through local sources to at least 100 liters per capita per day (Jal Dhara 2010, 2001). The main project of surface water is the Narmada Based Project or Sardar Sarovar Based Drinking Water Master Plan. When depletion and degradation was noticed in groundwater then it was decided in the year 1990-91 (Ninth Plan) to use water from Narmada to provide dependable water supply to the regions of Kutch, Saurashtra and North Gujarat.

A project called Sardar Sarovar Canal Based Drinking Water Supply Project was therefore designed to provide water supply to 8,215 villages and 135 towns of North Gujarat, Saurashtra and other parts of the state. The main objectives of the project are as follows:

1. To supply adequate and safe drinking water to the areas suffering from severe shortage of water supply.
2. To feed the regional water supply schemes, which are not providing adequate water supply due to failure of their respective sources.

3. To provide water supply to those regional schemes and individual (village) schemes which provide poor quality of water supply due to various reasons.
4. To supply potable water to those towns and villages which have excess salinity, excess fluoride or excess nitrates in their water supply.
5. To recharge ground water in depleted areas and to ensure drinking water to problem areas even during drought years.
6. To reduce out migration of people by ensuring drinking water and by promoting employment in the areas suffering from water shortages.

The implementation of the project has been spread over three phases: (i) Immediate Phase, which includes the most problematic districts of Amreli, Bhavnagar, Rajkot, Surendranagar and Kachchh; (ii) Phase I covering the areas where the water supply is not so frequent and also ground water is partially available. These areas include Panchmahal, Sabarkantha Banaskantha and Surendranagar; and (iii) Phase II covering all the remaining areas that fall under the project.

Water supply system of Gujarat aims to supply drinking water to 75 percent of the population of the state by creating bulk water transmission pipelines, water treatment plants, service reservoirs, distribution pipeline network and allied structures. The mission is to ensure sustainable water supply and sanitation services in the rural and urban areas of Gujarat state for accomplishing the basic health and hygiene levels leading to socio-economic development, peace and happiness in the society. According to Census 2001, there were a total of 18,066 villages and 242 towns of the state inhabited by 5.06 crore people in Gujarat. The Government of Gujarat has implemented an ambitious master plan for creation of State-Wide Water Supply Grid for a long-term water supply programme for drought proofing and inter-basin water transfer from sustainable surface water sources to water scarce and quality affected areas to supply drinking water to almost 75 percent of the population of the state through surface or sub-surface sources.

The state government has adopted a policy of installing regional water pipeline to carry water to distant villages, located 100 km. to 200 km. or even 300 km. away. Total number of projects planned is 334 under the State Wide Water Supply Grid. Out of this, 175 projects are covering 3,250 km. bulk pipeline for 9,633 villages and 131 towns of Narmada Master Plan, being implemented under the Sardar Sarovar Canal Based Water Supply Project Programme and Sujalam Suphalam Yojna Programme respectively. We have noticed that 159 projects covering 4,408 village and 12 towns based on surface or sub-surface sources are being implemented under the rural water supply programme.

Coverage Area of Villages through Water Supply Schemes in North Gujarat

In North Gujarat, there are various surface and groundwater schemes for providing the drinking water. The main sources of the drinking water are Narmada Canal Based Water Supply Projects, Regional Water Supply Schemes, Individual Pipe Water Supply Projects and Hand Pump Scheme. The Simple Well is not in use in North Gujarat. Basically, Regional Water Supply Schemes and Individual Piped Water Supply Projects depend on groundwater (Table 11.3).

All the villages of North Gujarat are covered under various schemes. Narmada Canal Based Water Supply Project is the main project of this region and 59 percent villages are covered under this project. Second large scheme is the Regional Water Supply Scheme and it has covered 35 percent of the total villages. The Handpump Scheme is working in two districts of Sabarkantha and Banaskantha. The Individual Pipeline Water Supply Project is not covering the two districts Mehsana and Patan. Most of the villages of Sabarkantha and Banaskantha district are covered with the Regional Water Supply Schemes and Individual Piped Water supply Schemes.

Table 11.3: Coverage Area through Various Schemes

District	Total No. of Villages	Villages Covered					
		Narmada Canal Based Water Supply Project	Regional Water Supply Scheme	Individual Piped Water Supply Project	Hand Pump Scheme	Simple Well	Total
Mehsana	593	464	129	0	0	0	593
Sabarkantha	1372	271	330	351	420	0	1372
Banaskantha	1244	470	392	342	40	0	1244
Patan	517	421	96	0	0	0	517
North Gujarat	2726	1626	947	693	460	0	2726
Gujarat	18066	6875	3983	4501	2627	80	18066

Source: GWSSB (2011).

Coverage of Town through Water Supply Schemes in North Gujarat

There are three types of schemes which cover almost all towns of North Gujarat. Gujarat has 242 towns and 11.5 percent of the towns are in North Gujarat (Table 11.4).

Narmada Canal Based Wafer Supply Project covers 63 percent of towns in North Gujarat followed by 15 percent towns by Regional Water Supply Scheme and 22 percent towns are covered by Individual Piped Water Supply Projects. Mehsana district covers 41 percent of the towns by the Narmada Canal Based Water Supply Project. Not a single town is covered by the Individual Piped Water Supply Project in Patan and Mehsana. Sabarkantha is covering 66 percent of the town under the Individual Piped Water Supply Project. Patan is the only district where only Narmada Canal Based Water Supply Projects is running. The total town coverage of North Gujarat is 15 percent by Narmada Canal Based Water Supply Project as compared to 66 percent covered by the Regional Water Supply Scheme and only 5 percent of the towns are covered by the Individual Piped Water Supply Project of North Gujarat.

Table 11.4: Coverage Area through Various Schemes

District	Total No. of Towns	Towns Covered			
		Narmada Canal Based Water Supply Project	Regional Water Supply Scheme	Individual Piped Water Supply Project	Total
Mehsana	8	7	1	0	8
Sabarkantha	8	3	1	4	8
Banaskantha	6	2	2	2	6
Patan	5	5	0	0	5
North Gujarat	27	17	4	6	27
Gujarat	242	114	13	115	242

Source: GWSSB (2011).

Sardar Sarovar Canal Based Drinking Water Supply Project

There are two types of surface water sources supply in the North Gujarat—Narmada Main Canal and other branches of small Narmada canals. The pumping station of the Narmada main canal is in Modhera (Table 11.5).

A total of 167 villages of Mehsana and 58 villages of Patan have been covered by the pumping stations. The water of Narmada Main Canal is supplied by the GWIL. 28 percent of the villages of Mehsana district and 11 percent villages of Patan district have been covered through the Narmada main canal.

The role of Narmada branch canal is important for the drinking water supply. The drinking water supply is managed by the GWSSB. A total of 38 percent villages are covered through Narmada branch canals in North Gujarat. All four districts are the beneficiaries of this surface water source. Most of the villages depend on Narmada branch canals.

Table 11.5: SSCB Drinking Water Supply Projects (Source-wise)

<table>
<tr><th colspan="2">Canal Off-takes</th><th>District</th><th>No. of Villages Covered</th><th>No. of Towns Covered</th></tr>
<tr><td rowspan="2">Water Supplied by GWIL</td><td rowspan="2">Narmada Main Canal (Modhera)</td><td>Mehsana</td><td>167</td><td>2</td></tr>
<tr><td>Patan</td><td>58</td><td>1</td></tr>
<tr><td rowspan="4">Water Supplied by GWSSB</td><td rowspan="4">From Narmada canals to Irrigation Infrastructure (irrigation pipelines-ponds and dam to be filled with Narmada water)</td><td>Mehsana</td><td>297</td><td>5</td></tr>
<tr><td>Patan</td><td>363</td><td>4</td></tr>
<tr><td>Banaskantha</td><td>470</td><td>2</td></tr>
<tr><td>Sabarkantha</td><td>271</td><td>3</td></tr>
</table>

Source: GWSSB (2011).

Sardar Sarovar Canal Based Drinking Water Supply Project (Beneficiary Population)

The total beneficiary population is 6.64 lacs in Mehsana district and 1.53 lacs in Patan district from Narmada main canal managed by GWIL. Approximately 40.09 lac of population beneficiaries are from all four districts which are managed by GWSSB (Table 11.6).

The major beneficiaries from water provided by GWIL are in Mehsana district. A total of 4.86 lacs people are the beneficiaries in Mehsana district followed by 1.34 lacs in Patan district. GWSSB is also providing the surface water to the maximum population in Mehsana. A total of 11.62 lac people are the beneficiaries in Mehsana district followed by 10.91 lac people in Banaskantha, 10.01 lac in Patan district and 6.55 lac in Sabarkantha district.

Table 11.6: Beneficiary Population Due to GWIL and GWSSB

Canal Off-takes		District	Beneficiary Population (in lacs)		
			Rural	Urban	Total
Water Supplied by GWIL	Narmada Main Canal (Modhera)	Mehsana	4.86	1.78	6.64
		Patan	1.34	0.19	1.53
Water Supplied by GWSSB	From Narmada canals to Irrigation Infrastructure (irrigation pipelines-ponds and dam to be filled with Narmada water)	Mehsana	8.70	2.92	11.62
		Patan	7.34	2.67	10.01
		Banaskantha	9.17	1.74	10.91
		Sabarkantha	5.39	1.15	6.55

Source: GWSSB (2011).

A total of 78 percent of the population in Mehsana district and 22 percent of the population in Patan district are using the surface water supplied by the GWSSB. The main source of the GWSSB is Narmada main canal. GWSSB is providing the surface water to all four districts of North Gujarat.

Conclusion

A comprehensive picture on the different sources of drinking and domestic water as supplied at the village level has been presented in this paper. It is to be noted that apart from the growing preference for surface water distribution system, the traditional water source is decreasing. Almost all the villages are covered by the government public water schemes and a huge amount of money has been invested for providing the safe water with the help of surface water. The water supply projects belong to the Narmada canal. Large numbers of villages are getting the Narmada water, but the major part of

North Gujarat is dependent on groundwater by various Regional and Individual pipeline schemes. Most of the villages in Mehsana and Patan have been covered with the Narmada Canal Based Water Supply Scheme. A large number of villages in Banaskantha and Sabarkantha are under the schemes of groundwater water supply because of their geographical location.

North Gujarat totally depends on the public water supply system but in the near future it may happen that the demand of the water could increase due to increase in population. Various problems could also arise in form of lack of availability of surface water and mismanagement in the supply system. If these types of expected problems are not solved immediately, then it is not only good for North Gujarat but Gujarat and India as well.

References

Census of India (2011), District-wise population of Gujarat, Office of the Registrar General and Census Commissioner, Ministry of Home Affairs, New Delhi, Government of India.

Hirway, I. (2004), Ensuring Drinking Water to All: A Study of Gujarat, Working Paper, Anand, IWMI.

RGNDWM (2010), National Rural Drinking Water Programme-Movement towards Ensuring People's Drinking Water Security in Rural India, Department of Drinking Water Supply, Government of India.

Socio-Economic Review (2011), Socio-Economic Review 2010-2011, Gujarat State, Budget Publication No. 34, Directorate of Economics and Statistics, Gandhinagar, Government of Gujarat.

12

Impact of Foreign Aid on Environmental Quality in India

Kalpana Sahoo and Narayan Sethi

Introduction

That foreign aid inflows influence the environment quality in developing countries, is not a new line of investigation. In the current dynamic world, most of the countries have been struggling hard to increase the per capita income by increasing the total output to sustain the competition. Overemphasis on achieving fast economic growth, however, puts severe threat to the environment quality and conveys fear for the availability of the natural resources for the future generations. India is the second largest growing economies of the world. In India, rapid economic growth has taken place over the last two decades by the adoption of economic reforms, heavy industrialization and acceptance of many developmental projects. These projects have been responsible for the degradation of the dense forest areas and have also caused massive loss of biodiversity. Weak implementation of environmental regulations has caused severe environmental damages in the form of air, water and soil pollutions. The degradation of environment in terms of environmental pollution, depletion of natural resources and loss of biodiversity are responsible for the reduction in income generation capacity of the present and future generations by affecting adversely their health status (Smith, 1999).

After the Second World War, hundreds of billions of foreign aid has been provided by the rich countries to the poor countries for welfare motives. Foreign aid is the international transfer of public funds in the form of loans and grants directly from one government or an international financial institution to another government at the time of need. It takes two forms such as loans at concessional terms (containing grant element of at least 25 percent) and grants which are non-refundable (OECD, 2009). The purpose of the foreign aid program is to accelerate the process of economic development up to a point where a satisfactory rate of growth can be achieved on a self-sustaining basis. However, in the current scenario, environmental degradation has become one of the greatest challenges for the mankind.

The traditional approach of measuring the effectiveness of foreign aid through growth dimension of the given country is no longer considered as a sufficient criterion. Presently, the effectiveness of aid programs is evaluated by considering its impact on environmental protection, stable political economy and sustainable development. Hatzipanayotou, Lahiri, and Michael (2002) developed a two country model of aid and cross-border pollution resulting from production activities in the recipient country. Their study found that the impact of cross-border pollution leads to reduction in the total amount of emissions by encouraging higher amount of international financial assistance. This study has suggested that performance-driven aid transfers approach should be used in the pollution policy in the polluting country to protect the environment.

In the era of globalization, economies are so dependent on each other that impact of one economy quickly affects the other economy. Pollution does not respect national boundaries affecting both the polluters as well as other countries across the world. Environmental pollution is a matter of concern for both polluted and clean economies as the productivity of an individual country is affected by the worldwide aggregate emission of harmful materials (Branden and Bromley, 1981; Hoel, 1991; Dockner and Long, 1993). The impact of foreign aid on improving the global environmental quality depends on the marginal rate of substitution between the environmental qualities of the trading partners and the relative efficiency in the technology of reducing pollution in the recipient country to that in the donor country (Niho, 1996). In recent years, most of the developing countries would have experienced a lower rate of growth in terms of reduction of poverty and pollution if the amount of foreign aid had been reduced (Addison et al., 2004). Lack of adequate funds for environmental clean-up and preservation is one of the major factors responsible for environmental degradation in many poorer countries. In this context, aid has a role to control such degradation and to protect the environment, particularly in the poor countries.

Capital is the life blood of all the economic activities. Shortage of capital is a common feature of all the developing countries. There are two major sources which help in the generation of capital i.e., internal sources and external sources. Internal sources include domestic capital formation which is a combination of household savings, private savings and government savings and the revenue generated through taxation. The main forms of external capital inflows are official flows and private flows. Official capital flows refers to the transfer of resources at a concessional rate from a developed country or an international financial institution to a poor nation. It includes foreign aid, grants, and other assistances. Private capital flows includes all the investments made by foreign companies, firms and individuals in various sectors of the economy. The major difference between these two types of flows is that the former is guided by the welfare motive, whereas the latter is guided by the profit motive. Hence, private capital flows has nothing to do with the developmental programs like infrastructural development, education, health, environment preservation etc. of the poor countries. Foreign capital in terms of aid is the other alternate available with the poor countries to supplement its scarce domestic capital. Some theoretical studies find that foreign aid inflows may not only reduce poverty but also encourage preservation of natural resources by the poorer nations.

The environmental Kuznets curve (EKC) argues that pollution levels rise in the early stages of development but recede subsequently. Asafu-Adjaye (1999) has supported the main thrust of environmental Kuznets curve and also found that turning points of the curve vary by both country and pollutant type. Some empirical studies have emerged in recent years relating to this aid and its impact on environment quality. Arvin et al. (2006) examined the relationship between foreign aid and ecological conditions in developing countries using a Granger causality test, while Arvin and Lew (2007) examined the same nexus in a broader model by considering some other determinants that affect environmental conditions.

The present study broadly examines the impact and causal dynamic relationship between foreign aid and environment quality in India over the period 1970-71 to 2010-11. By using the Granger causality technique, the present study aims to determine the causal linkage between foreign aid and major macroeconomic variables with the environmental quality in India. The present study tries to verify whether aid inflows influence the environment quality in India, whether the environment affects aid inflows to India or whether causality persists in both directions. The remaining part of this paper discusses the introduction; current environmental conditions in India with comparison to some other developed and developing nations; nature, sources and methodology of the study; analysis of the empirical results and its discussion; and the summary and conclusion.

Environment Quality, Foreign Aid and Economic Growth in India

Currently, India is considered as one of the most emerging economic powers of the world. It was not much affected by the global financial crisis of 2007-08 like other developed nations. If we compare GDP growth rate of India then it is quite higher in the post-Crisis period but at the same time if we compare the other developmental indicators, then it is quite unfavourable for its economy. Since the Industrial Revolution, human activities have had a substantial impact on environment quality. Most significantly, the burning of fossil fuels, heavy industrialization, use of harmful products, machineries and equipments, use of heavy chemicals in agriculture, extraction of contaminated water supply, desertification, urbanization and deforestation are some of the major factors responsible for environment degradation. These factors raise the amount of greenhouse gases which causes climate change, global warming and ozone layer depletion.

According to the Fourth Assessment Report of the Intergovernmental Panel on Climate Change (IPCC, 2007), over the century, atmospheric concentrations of carbon dioxide increased from a pre-industrial value of 278 parts per million to 379 parts per million in 2005, and the average global temperature rose by 0.740°C (Economic Survey, 2011). Table 12.1 shows top 10 richest countries in the world which are classified on the basis of the GDP (nominal), 2011. The table also shows the release of carbon dioxide emissions (in million tons) and environment vulnerability index (EVI) of these top 10 richest countries in the world. EVI is a measurement devised by the South Pacific Applied Geoscience Commission (SOPAC) and the United Nations Environment Programs to characterize the relative severity of various types of environment issues.

From Table 12.1, it is clear that USA is the richest country in the world. It also occupies first position in releasing CO_2 emissions i.e. 2,530 MT which is followed by China, Russia and India. India occupies 10th position in terms of nominal GDP, but it ranks 4th position in releasing carbon dioxide emissions which is the main cause of environment pollution, global warming and ozone layer depletion. In case of environment vulnerability index, India's position is extremely vulnerable in comparison to other countries of the world. It clearly shows India's position on preservation of environment is not satisfactory.

Table 12.1: List of Top 10 Richest Countries in the World (GDP, Nominal), 2011

Richest Country (Nominal GDP)	CO_2 Emissions (mt.)	Environment Vulnerability Index (EVI)
USA	2,530	300 (Vulnerable)
China	2,430	360 (Highly Vulnerable)
Japan	363	389 (Extremely Vulnerable)
Germany	323	357(Highly Vulnerable)
France	315	361(Highly Vulnerable)
Brazil	205	281 (Vulnerable)
UK	192	373 (Extremely Vulnerable)
Italy	201	273 (Vulnerable)
Russia	600	273 (Vulnerable)
India	569	385 (Extremely Vulnerable)

Source: CIA World Factbook.

Table 12.2 shows the list of top seven countries across world in case of highest population, greatest water pollutants and countries with highest nuclear weapons. The Table shows that India is the second largest populated country following China. In terms of greatest water pollutants, India occupies third position following China and USA. In terms of having the maximum nuclear weapons in the world, India occupies the 7th position.

Table 12.2: List of Top 7 Most Populous Countries in the World, 2011

Most Populous Countries	Greatest Water Polluter	Countries with Most Nuclear Weapons
China	China	Russia
India	USA	USA
USA	India	France
Indonesia	Japan	China
Brazil	Germany	UK
Pakistan	Indonesia	Israel
Nigeria	Brazil	India

Source: CIA World Factbook.

India ranks in the top ten in terms of green house gas (GHG) emissions. This high level of emissions is contributed by its large population, heavy industrialization, urbanization, deforestation and geographical size. The Indian Network for Climate Change Assessment (INCCA, 2010) has found that the total net GHG emissions from India in 2007 were 1727.71 million tons (carbon dioxide emissions were 1221.76 million tons; methane 20.56 million tons; and nitrous oxide 0.24 million tons) in comparison to 1228.54 million tons in 1994. This represents a compounded annual growth rate of 2.9 percent during the period 1994 to 2007. GHG emissions from the energy, industry, agriculture and waste sectors in 2007 constituted 58 percent, 22 percent, 17 percent and 3 percent of the net CO_2 emissions respectively (Economic Survey, 2011).

Economic development without environmental considerations can cause serious environmental damage by affecting the quality of life of present and future generations. This challenges needs to be addressed in the economic planning, with necessary remedial measures. Recognizing the importance of taking corrective measures to protect the environment, Government of India, through its various policies, has been adopting some ecological concerns into the development process so that economic development can be achieved without damaging the environment. Table 12.3 shows some recent initiative measures adopted by Government of India with an aim to protect the environment quality.

Methodology and Model Specification

The present study empirically examines the impact of foreign aid on environment quality in India from 1970-71 to 2010-11. This study uses variables like gross domestic product (GDP as the indicator of economic growth), official development assistance (ODA, as an indicator of foreign assistance), population (popu), external debt (ED), trade openness (TL, as an indicator of liberalization), urbanization

(URB) and carbon dioxide emissions (CO_2), as an indicator of environment pollution) for its empirical analysis.

Table 12.3: Recent Initiatives/Measures for Environment Protection by Government of India

Measure	Objective
The Wetlands (Conservation and Management) Rules 2010	Ensure the degradation of wetlands from industrialization, construction, dumping of untreated waste
The National Green Tribunal (NGT) Act, 2010	Relating to environmental protection and conservation of forests and other natural resources
The Coastal Regulation Zone Notification, 6th January, 2011	To protect coastal ecosystems which protect biodiversity and also saves from natural disasters such as floods and tsunamis
Integrated Coastal Zone Management Project, 1156 cr. (with World Bank)	This project is for a period of five years. It is estimated that it will benefit 3.56 crore people directly 6.30 crore indirectly.
National Action Plan on Climate Change (NAPCC), June, 2008	Sustainable development

Source: Economic Survey, 2011.

The whole study is based on the secondary annual time series data which is collected from the World Development Indicators published by the World Bank and Economic Survey of India. This study uses the statistical package E-views 5.0 for its empirical analysis. Three variables i.e. ODA, ED and TL are expressed in terms of US$ except population (in million), and CO_2 (in mt.). GDP and urbanization are expressed in terms of their annual growth rate. The study use CO_2 as the indicator of environment quality. Due to high variation in their absolute values, variables like ODA, ED and TL are expressed as a percentage of GDP. This study makes use of some simple econometric methods to carry out the empirical analysis. We use the Granger causality test for our empirical analysis.

First, we calculate the descriptive statistics for all the variables. The causal dynamic relationship between foreign aid on environment quality in India may be examined by using the concept of Granger-causality test. Granger's causality proposed by Granger (1969) and popularized by Sims (1972) may be defined as the forecasting relationship between two variables.

Before using the Granger causality test, one should test the stationary properties of the variable in case of time series data. As our data is time series in nature, the study needs to test stationarity of the variables using unit root tests, namely Augmented-Dicky Fuller (ADF), Phillips-Perron (PP) (1988) and Kwiatkowski-Phillips-Schmidt-Shin (KPSS) tests to avoid the spurious regression results.

Among the three unit root tests, only the KPSS test without trend shows the stationarity of all the variables (see Table 12.4). Granger causality test states that if E and F are two time series variables and, if past values of a variable E significantly contribute to forecast the value of the other variable F, then E is said to be Granger causing F and vice-versa. The test involves the following two regression equations:

$$E_t = \gamma_0 + \sum_{i=1}^{n} \alpha_i F_{t-i} + \sum_{j-1}^{n} \beta_j E_{t-j} + u_{1t} \tag{1}$$

$$F_t = \gamma_1 + \sum_{i=1}^{m} \lambda_i E_{t-i} + \sum_{j=1}^{n} \delta_j + F_{t-j} + u_{2t} \tag{2}$$

Here,

Et and F_t are foreign aid and environment quality respectively,

u_{1t} and u_{2t} are mutually uncorrelated white noise errors,

t denotes the time period.

Equation 1 proposes that current E is related to past values of E as well as of past F. Similarly, equation 2 postulates that F is related to past values of F as well as related to past values of E. Three possible conclusions can be drawn from Granger causality test viz., unidirectional causality, bi-directional causality and no causality that they are independent of each other.

Table 12.4: Unit Root Test Results

Variables	ADF		PP		KPSS	
	Without Trend	With Trend	Without Trend	With Trend	Without Trend	With Trend
CO_2	0.11	-2.31	0.66	-2.18	0.66**	0.2**
ODA	-1.81	-0.74	-2.14	-2.87	0.72**	0.23*
POPU	-2.83***	-1.44	1.56	-5.66*	0.74*	0.19**
GDP	-5.44*	-7.5*	-5.4*	-8.5*	0.77*	0.07
TL	-2.53	-2.99	-2.54	-2.99	0.37**	0.6
URB	-5.65*	-3.12	-0.68	-1.5	0.75*	0.18*
ED	-2.64***	-2.83	-1.73	-1.51	0.27***	0.16**

Source: Author's Calculation by using E-views 5.0 Software.

Notes: The critical values for unit root tests are 0.739, 0.463 and 0.347 without trend in KPSS.

*, ** and *** indicate significance at 1 percent, 5 percent and 10 percent level respectively.

Empirical Results

This section deals with the analysis of the empirical results and its discussion. The empirical result is calculated by using the Granger-Causality test. Before going to use the Granger-causality test, the present study has examined the stationary property of the time series data. After that, the descriptive statistics of the variables has been calculated. Next it has used the Granger causality test to measure the dynamic causal relationship between foreign aid on environment quality.

This study has used annual time series data of 41 years which contains some trend. Before using any econometric technique in any time series data, the first step is to identify whether the series is stationary or not. If the variables of a time series data do not satisfy the stationary property, then the regression result may be a spurious one. Unit root test is used to test the stationary property of the variables. Stationarity of the variables are very much desired, as non-stationary series will produce spurious regression estimates and the resulting outcome will be of no practical use.

Unit root test is a pre-requisite of testing long-run relationship between two or more time series data (Granger, 1981). Augmented Dickey-Fuller (ADF), Phillips-Perron (PP) and Kwiatkowski-Phillips-Schmidt-Shin (KPSS) tests are widely used in empirical research. Here, to test the stationarity of the variables, we conducted all the three tests. The criterion of selection for unit test was that the absolute value of the test statistics should be higher than the critical value of the variables. The result of unit root test has shown in Table 12.4. The test results suggest that all the variables are stationary in KPSS without trend.

Table 12.5 shows the results of descriptive statistics. The mean values of the ED, ODA and CO_2 are similar to some extent. The variability present among the variables is measured by the standard deviation. From the descriptive statistics result, it is clear that the variability among the variables is different to each other. The maximum and the minimum values show the range in between which the values of the variables are lying. Here, all the values of the variables are lying in between -5.23 to 9.8. Skewness helps us to determine the nature and extent of the concentration of the observations towards the highest or the lowest values of the variables. The skewness values of ODA, ED and URB are positive which indicates that the frequency curve of all the distributions are not symmetric bell shaped curve rather they are stretched more to the right side or have a longer tail towards the right side. Rest four variables are negatively skewed. Kurtosis is concentrated with the flatness or peakedness of the frequency curve. The kurtosis values of all the variables except GDP are less than 3, which shows that all the variables (except GDP) have platykurtic curve (less peaked than normal curve).

Table 12.5: Descriptive Statistics Result

	ODA	CO_2	ED	GDP
Mean	2.33	2.84	2.28	5.53968
Median	1.37	3.06	2.19	5.708653
Maximum	7.93	3.52	3.62	9.817004
Minimum	1.24	1.89	1.30	-5.23759
Std. Dev.	2.36	5.00	6.51	3.141423
Skewness	1.01	-0.782	0.587	-1.06965
Kurtosis	2.84	2.131	2.319	4.723009
Jarque-Bera	7.024459	5.472123	3.148095	12.88995
Probability	0.02983	0.064825	0.207205	0.001588
Sample Size	41	41	41	41

Contd...

	POPU	TL	URB
Mean	1.990136	-0.70318	1.42
Median	2.090642	-0.62171	1.12
Maximum	2.371483	2.304306	3.20
Minimum	1.387478	-3.68621	2.41
Std. Dev.	0.339339	1.341094	1.00
Skewness	-0.46301	-0.23816	0.503
Kurtosis	1.71227	2.797579	1.788
Jarque-Bera	4.297775	0.457572	4.239475
Probability	0.116614	0.795499	0.120063
Sample Size	41	41	41

Source: Author's Calculation by using E-views 5.0 Software.

Choice of Lag Length: Before going for the Granger causality test, one must have to select the appropriate lag length of the time series data. While determining lag length, econometricians have either fixed the lag length arbitrarily or chosen it through some statistical procedure. The study uses five lag order selection criterion such as likelihood ratio (LR), final prediction error (FPE), Akaike information criterion (AIC), Schwarz information criterion (SC) and Hannan-Quinn information criterion (HQ). Here, all the five criteria unanimously select lag order 3 (Table 12.6), and thus, we take 3 as the optimum lag length. A lag of three years seems appropriate to analyze the relationship between foreign aid inflows and environment quality in India.

Table 12.6: Choice of Lag Length Criteria

Lag	LR	FPE	AIC	SC	HQ
0	NA	7.14E-77	-155.469	-155.167	-155.361
1	520.1369	2.91E-83	-170.228	-167.814	-169.369
2	114.202	3.51E-84	-172.614	-168.089	-171.004
3	92.12183*	3.35e-85*	-175.7925*	-169.1560*	-173.4313*

Notes: * indicates lag order selected by the criterion.
LR: sequential modified LR test statistic (each test at 5 percent level), FPE: Final prediction error, AIC: Akaike information criterion, SC: Schwarz information criterion, HQ: Hannan-Quinn information criteria.

Granger Causality Test Result: The study has used the Granger causality test to find the dynamic causal relationship between foreign aid and environment quality. Since the reliability of the Granger causality test results depends on stationary of the variables, it has used the ADF, PP and KPSS test. The result of unit root test (Table 12.4) shows that all the variables are stationary at KPSS (without trend). It is well-known that Granger causality test is sensitive to the choice of lag length.

The major findings of the pair-wise Granger causality test are discussed here. The most important observation is that there is a positive bidirectional causal relationship that exists between economic growth (GDP) with environment pollution (CO_2), foreign aid (ODA) and urbanization growth. It clearly shows that economic growth has direct positive impact on the above three variables. This result finds that both GDP and CO_2 emissions affect each other which indicates that higher rate of economic growth causes more environmental pollution.

There is also a bi-directional causal relationship observed between urbanization growth rate and CO_2 emissions, which means higher growth of urbanization leads to more environmental pollution in India. Adding to this, is the unidirectional causal relationship observed in case of population growth and CO_2 emissions which indicates that population growth leads to more environmental pollution in India. In this study, all the unidirectional causal relation has shown positive causal relation except the impact of foreign aid on CO_2 emissions. The results show that there is negative unidirectional relationship that exists between foreign aid and CO_2 emissions which specifies that foreign aid is inversely related with CO_2 gas emissions in India during the study period. It implies that foreign aid has significant but negative impact on CO_2 gas emissions in India during the study period. There is no causal relationship that exists between trade liberalization on CO_2 emissions, foreign aid, urbanization and population growth. That means these variables are independent of each other. No causal relationship exists between these pair-wise variables.

Conclusions

This paper contributes to the recent empirical literature of aid effectiveness. This paper empirically analyses the causal dynamic relationship between foreign aid on environment pollution using the Granger causality test for India over the period 1970-71 to 2010-11. The empirical results show that there is a unidirectional relation that exists between foreign aid and environment quality in India. The study concludes that the impact of aid on environment pollution is negative and significant—indicates aid helps in reduction of environmental pollution and indirectly helps in the preservation of the environment quality. This study confirms to the findings given by Arvin and Lew (2007) that foreign aid helps in the reduction of CO_2 gas emissions in the recipient country. The study also finds that higher rate of economic growth, urbanization and heavy population pressure are some of the major determinants of increasing CO_2 gas emissions in India during the study period. These factors contributed to the degradation of environment quality in India in terms of releasing more GHGs to the environment, polluting the water bodies by adding contaminated water extracted from industries and reducing the productivity of the land by using harmful chemicals.

Higher economic growth and good environment quality are two important criteria for survival of the mankind and also to live a healthy life with dignity. Therefore, both should be given equal importance by the Government of India. The ultimate objective of development planning is increasing social welfare and well-being of the people. Increased social welfare of the people requires a more equitable distribution of development benefits along with better living environment. Hence, it is the responsibility of the government to make appropriate plans with the aim to maintain a balance between growth challenges and environmental challenges. The rising importance of environment-related issues should not hamper the foundations of our inclusive growth strategy. Careful planning and systematic policies should be implemented to ensure that the green growth strategies do not result in a slow growth strategy. However, the study is not without its limitations. The study is constrained due to the unavailability of time series data of certain variables like environment aid, polluted water quality, land degradation and deforestation. The present study can hopefully provoke further empirical research to find out the impact of specific environment aid on both environment quality and economic growth in India.

References

Addison, T., Mavrotas, G. and McGillivray M. (2004), Aid, Alternative Sources of Finance and the Millennium Development Goals, Paper presented at the Development Studies Association's Annual Conference, London, November.

Arvin, B.M., Dabir-Alai, P. and Lew, B. (2006), Does Foreign Aid Affect the Environment in Developing Economies?", *Journal of Economic Development*, 31, pp. 63-87.

Arvin, B.M. and Lew, B. (2007), Can Foreign Assistance Bring Better Air Quality to Developing Countries?", *International Journal of Applied Business and Economic Research*, 5, pp. 31-37.

Asafu-Adjaye, J. (1999), The Environment and Development: Theory and Empirical Evidence, *International Journal of Development Planning Literature*, 14, pp. 117-134.

Branden, J.B. and Bromley, D. (1981), The Economics of Cooperation Over Collective Bads, *Journal of Environmental Economics and Management*, 8, pp. 134-150.

Dicky, D.A and Fuller W.A. (1981), Likehood Ratio Statistics for Autoregressive Time Series with a Unit Root, *Econometrica*, 49, pp. 1057-1072.

Dockner, E.J. and Long N.V. (1993), International Pollution Control: Cooperative versus Non-Cooperative Strategies, *Journal of Environmental Economics and Management*, 25, pp. 13-29.

Economic Survey (2010-11), Government of India.

Granger, C.W.J. (1981), Some Properties of Time Series Data and Their Uses in Econometric Model Specification, *Journal of Econometrics,* 16.

Gujarati, Damodar N. (2004), Basic Econometrics, (4th Edition), McGraw Hill.

Handbook of Statistics on Indian Economy (2011), Reserve Bank of India.

Hatzipanayotou, P., Lahiri, S. and Michael M.S. (2002), Can Cross-Border Pollution Reduce Pollution?", *Canadian Journal of Economics*, 35, pp. 805-818.

Hoel, M. (1991), Global Environmental Problems: The Effect of Unilateral Actions Taken by One Country, *Journal of Environmental Economics and Management*, 20, pp. 55-70.

Niho, Y. (1996), Effects of an International Income Transfer on the Global Environmental Quality, *Japan and the World Economy*, 8, pp. 401-410.

Pedersen, Karl R. (1996), Aid, Investment and Incentives, *Scandinavian Journal of Economics*, 98(3), pp. 423-438.

Phillips, P.C.B. and Perron P. (1988), Testing for Unit Root in Time Series Regression, *Biometrica*, pp. 335-346.

Smith, James P. (1999), Healthy Bodies and Thick Wallets: The Dual Relation between Health and Social-economic Status, *Journal of Economic Perspectives*, 13, pp. 145-166.

World Bank (2011), World Development Indicators, (online database).

Index

Index